# The Complete Book of Fishing Knots, Leaders, and Lines

Lindsey Philpott

WITHDRAWN

HARFORD COUNTY
PUBLIC LIBRARY
100 E. Pennsylvania Avenue
Bel Air, MD 21014

Skyhorse Publishing

Skyhorse Publishing books may be purchased in bulk at special discounts for sales promotion, corporate gifts, fund raising, or educational purposes. Special editions can also be created to specifications. For details, contact Special Sales Department, Skyhorse Publishing, 555 Eighth Avenue, Suite 903, New York, NY 10018 or info@skyhorsepublishing.com.

www.skyhorsepublishing.com

10 9 8 7 6 5 4 3 2 1

Library of Congress Cataloging-in-Publication Data

Philpott, Lindsey.
   The complete book of fishing knots, leaders, and lines / Lindsey Philpott.
      p. cm.
   Includes bibliographical references and index.
   ISBN-13: 978–1–60239–224–3 (pbk. : alk. paper)
   ISBN-10: 1–60239–224–2 (pbk. : alk. paper)
   1. Fishing knots. 2. Leaders (Fishing) 3. Fishing lines. I. International Game Fish Association. II. Title.
   SH452.9.K6P45 2008
   799.12—dc22
                              2007050476

Printed in China

# Contents

# Acknowledgments

The author is greatly indebted to the following for their advice, encouragement, and leadership, particularly in allowing the author free rein with his sometimes scattered and witless rantings about knots. To my wife, Kim, for having the tenacity and forbearance to put up with me; to my sons Nick and Ben for their able and willing assistance, especially Ben who took many of the photographs you see here; to my friend and knotting companion, Jimmy Ray Williams, who also was kind enough to lend his skills in taking photographs throughout the book; to the Joes, Charlies, Toms, Gordons, Jeffs, Kens, and countless others of the International Guild of Knot Tyers both here and abroad, who have by their own efforts far outstripped any small efforts I have made; and to all those to whom I have made mention of my passion, knotting, and who have nodded sagely and then wisely stepped aside to allow me to get on with it. Last, but by no means least, the author wishes to thank the understanding and forbearing editorial and publishing crew at Skyhorse for having brought so much gold out of so much dross. Thank you all.

# Chapter 1

# What You Need to Know About Knots

*· Knot Terminology   · How Knots Work   · How to Work with Line   · How to Finish the Line   · What Not to Do*

As anglers we are the first to admit that we have favorite fishing knots for different situations, and only those knots will do—we swear by them and would not change for all the tea in China. We grow accustomed to tying a particular knot in the type of line we prefer and do not want to change our familiar methods. Because we have this history with knots and line, we have definite ideas about which knots and lines work best and where they work best, so what could there possibly be that you need to know about the subject? Read on.

Tying knots in line, particularly slick line like monofilament, has always been a challenge. All record-setting anglers agree that they had to learn their knots first, along with a thorough familiarity of lines and other equipment. It is neither staying out of the weeds and rocks, finding the perfect bait, nor even staying out of the trees or snags that presents the record seeker with the greatest challenge. At the outset, tying good, reliable knots is the greatest challenge. The line seems thin, slick, and fiddly—it seems to have a mind of its own. But it has to be mastered if you are to keep up with the record-setters. With practice, you can certainly master the necessary skills. With practice, you can show others those skills and go on to learn, or perhaps even invent your own knots.

When you are peacefully practicing knot tying you have all the time in the world. But see a rise and you have to know which knot to tie and you have to tie it now. Having learned and practiced ahead of time will serve you well. You will have confidence that the hook and line will remain together on that 20-pounder.

Here I'll present at least three of the secrets to tying good knots that stay tied. Practicing them before you go, seated in your comfy chair with this book at your side, will help you to gain skill and confidence.

The first secret to tying knots is no secret really—you have to pick the right knot, or the fish is lost before you make your first cast. If your knot looks ragged, it will snag before it hits the water. If your knot is lumpy, it will be visible to fish for miles—well, yards anyway. Worse yet, if your knot has to pass through small-diameter rod guides and you have tied the right knot, but in the wrong direction, you could end up spending valuable time untangling snarled line.

You should seek out advice wherever you can regarding which knots work best for what you doing. You have taken the right first step in picking up this book. Get advice from your fishing buddies, captains and guides, the storeowner where you get your tackle—they are all good sources of information. Just a friendly word though: don't rely on their advice alone. Consider what they are saying and make up your own mind.

The second secret that I want to share is that life does not stand still. You will have to grow with it, whether you want to or not. Fishing, as part of life, is not a sport that likes to stay still: it is constantly evolving. New lines are coming out all the time, new rods, new reels, new gear—there is always something new. Your knots, however, having stood the test of time, have not changed in maybe five or ten years, maybe even since you first tied them? So, do you think that maybe there is something you could stand to learn about knots, even if you choose not to use the information? If you can gain some greater understanding of how knots work, and in which kinds of line, wouldn't that be worth hanging onto? Before you answer, let's consider the third big secret.

When a New York cabbie was asked by a breathless young woman running to his taxi from Grand Central Station, with a violin case gripped white-knuckle tight in her hand, "What's the best way to get to Carnegie Hall?" he laconically replied, "Practice, practice, practice." It's not my joke, but that's my advice, in a nutshell, the third secret. You must practice or you will get to be like that garden rake you haven't used in years—rusty. When you do practice, try tying a new knot by first following all the directions. Then see if you can find some shortcuts or missed steps that you need to know about. Practice will help your fingers remember the moves, and once the moves are memorized, you may discover new and different ways of holding the line when tying the Blood Knot, or Bimini Twist, so that you do not let go at a crucial moment, or you do not twist something too much or too little. Remember that different line materials will affect the way a certain knot should be tied. Whether it is too many twists or too few—there is going to be something different about it, so be alert.

Before we get started in earnest, take a look at the complete Glossary of Terms toward the end of the book. Familiarity with the names for the parts of knots and line will help you get started. Here are a few critical ones.

## Knot Terminology

- **Line:** Any piece of flexible material made of man-made (usually) or organic (not much these days) fibers, used, in our case, for catching fish. It may also be a piece of wire, but don't let that fool you—it is still referred to as line.
- **Standing End** (also standing part): The main part of the line that is attached to the reel. Also, the part to which you are attempting to fix your leader or other piece of gear—it's the part that stands alone with nothing to do other than wait for you to attach something to it.
- **Wrap:** A complete circle around a standing part is one turn or wrap. If your line starts the wrap on the side away from you it should finish in the same position to make a round turn or wrap. The working end, or tag end should finish the wrap in the same place it started.
- **Tag End** (also working end): The end of your line that you are using to make the knot. Sometimes you make the tag end by cutting away a part of the line—it is still the tag end that remains in or under the knot, while the part you throw away is just that—the part you throw away. Be nice to your environment and don't throw it in the water—if you pack it in, pack it out.

- **Loop:** A loop is formed when the line crosses or meets itself. The difference between a loop and a bight is that a bight stays open, while a loop is closed.
- **Bight:** An open, U-shaped bend in a line, a bight is simply a part of the line that has been turned toward itself, but has neither crossed nor met itself. If you were to take a bite out of a piece of bread or cheese, the mark left is called a bight because of the U-shape.
- **Knot:** An easy one really—a knot is any tangle in a piece of flexible line. It could be wire, mono, or a piece of garden hose. Knots happen by accident or by design—let's try to make them all by design.
- **Bend:** When you attach one piece of line to another piece, you are making a bend or you are bending one line onto the other. This may seem confusing at first, but you will soon see what is meant from the tying descriptions.
- **Hitch:** When you want to attach a piece of line to something other than another piece of line (such as the reel arbor or a sinker) you would, strictly speaking, be using a hitch.
- **Splice:** To "marry" one piece of line to itself or to another piece of the same or different material. This usually involves weaving the individual parts of the line over and under each other, but may also involve the "trapped finger puzzle" trick, where one piece of line traps the inserted piece by gripping it. Splicing may also involve sticking one piece of line to another with glue— really. Be sure to take a look at the Glossary now.

At this point, let's think for a moment about how knots work, and then we can progress to what you should not do in tying knots— after that we'll be ready to start tying some knots. If you are there already and want to skip this part of the book, go ahead. Just don't blame me when you find that you should have read this bit first before you decided which knot to use.

## How Knots Work

Knots work by compression, tension or friction, allowing the line to slide to a pre-determined point and no further through their design. Compression is when the line squeezes against itself or against another object, such as a hook eye, so it will not slip. Tension is what happens when line is stretched, pulling against itself to remain tight. Too little tension makes a knot that is not seated, and will slip; too much tension can damage the knot and line and weaken it.

Friction is what happens when one line rubs against another, sometimes producing heat in the process. Friction can be a friend or a foe. If you are using slick line, like fluorocarbon, you need friction in the right place; if you are using thick line or wire, you need to know what knots will work best to reduce tension in the wrong places. When using monofilament you need to develop compression, so the knot stays tied. Understanding the structure and purpose of the knot is essential to getting the knot to work for you.

Many of the knots that we use for modern, flexible plastic (monofilament) lines have been adapted from knots developed to join cotton, linen, silkworm gut, wire or any number of materials. Most line today is synthetic and may have different qualities than the material for which the knots were originally developed. The type of line most commonly used is polyamide, known universally as nylon. Beyond that there is polyester, also known as Dacron. Then there are ultra-high molecular weight polyethylene or UHMWPE lines, known as Spectra, and polyvinylidenefluoride or PVDF, also known as fluorocarbon. When we attempt to tie a knot in one of these newer types of line, a standby knot that does well in other line material may not work so well. To work with knots and line, we have to know which kind of line we are dealing with. Each material has different characteristics, and we have to adapt our knots to work with each material. We will take a look at the types of line in the next chapter, but for now, let's take a look in more detail at the ways in which knots work.

To review, there are three principal ways in which knots work:

- Wrapping or compression, with and without loops,
- Tucking or tension, with and without loops,
- Tucking and wrapping combined to provide friction

There is a fourth way that knots work, and that is when one line is pinched by another, like those finger-puzzles that trap your finger until you release the tension. Essentially, I am classifying this type of knot structure, if you can call it that, as a wrapping-type, for obvious reasons. However, very few knots use this as the single method of being formed (as yet, anyway) and I shall not speak much of it from this point onwards, choosing instead to focus on the three principal methods.

Let's look at these three modes individually:

*Wrapping*

Wrapping a line is a good way of generating compression against itself or the object to which it is being tied. We need compression to get the two surfaces of the line to "stick" together. Wrapping involves making tight turns in succession, one after the other, so that there is plenty of contact between the wrapping line and the wrapped item. When you are wrapping a line, you have to keep it under tension or it will get away from you. You will need to practice the art of keeping one finger and/or thumb on the turns as you make them, so that they do not lose that tension that holds them in place. Another important factor in wrapping is that you will likely have to lubricate the knot to get it to tighten properly. You can wet the line by adding a few drops of water, or saliva.

If you are wrapping loops you'll also need to remember which part of the loop to pull to form the knot. Loops also have to be set against each other just right or they will not work, and could cut through each other.

Occasionally you will be making turns over previous turns, to gain even more friction—we are often dealing with monofilament, and some very slippery conditions, particularly when the knot is wet. Wraps have to have a tucked portion so the wraps stay put. The tucked part is just as important as the wrap in making the knot.

*Tucking*

When you are tucking a tag end or any part of the line, or perhaps a bight of line, remember to insert the loop from the side designated in the instructions. Trapping the end or bight in this way prevents it from pulling out of the knot or hitch—it keeps the line under tension. If the instructions say to enter from the top, this means to enter from the side of the knot that's facing you, pushing the tag or bight away from you. When the instructions say to enter from below, it means to insert the tag end or the bight into the loop or hitch from the side that is away from you, to come out of the loop or hitch towards you.

If the instructions say to tuck the line *over* the main line, don't try to tuck it *under*—it matters. It is also important to trap the line temporarily with your fingers at any point in the tying process where the knot might unravel.

*Wrapping and tucking together*
As the description suggests, we can combine the two methods above to get the best of the gripping of the turns and the trapping of the line. Both methods require you to apply some tension to the line and some lubrication, so be prepared, and be particularly aware of the hook point when it poses a threat to your fingers. Practice on dry land or when you are least stressed—it will help you to remember how to make the knot under stress when you see the action unfold and the knot must be tied quickly and properly.

Wrapping and following it up with a tuck involves sometimes making wraps outside what you might think of as the business end of the knot. This is done for a couple of reasons:

1. That's how it has worked in the past and,
2. See reason #1.

## How to Work with Line

Quite apart from how the knots themselves work, we need to understand something of how to work with line. In doing so, you can get the best match between knot and line.

1. Don't apply more tension to fair up the knot than the line is rated for. You would be amazed at the number of people who break their 4-pound-test line after making a successful knot, simply because they pulled too hard when tightening it.

2. Practice tying knots at home. The techniques you can use at home, however, may not always work when you are standing on a slippery riverbank or a tippy boat on choppy waters. Sometimes knots and leaders need to be prepared ahead of time, before you are on the water.

3. Keep your line in the dark when not in use. Sunlight affects the strength of fishing line.

4. Use the right size spool for the line you have chosen—it will do you no good to set up with 20-pound line for spinning if it will not come off the spool when you cast. Similarly, don't use light line on a large spool, unless you have a large wallet.

## How to Finish the Line

The tag ends of your line are mostly going to be finished with a clipper. Never burn the tag ends of your lines. Not only is the off-gas and smoke dangerous to inhale, the heat of burning plastic on your skin is a memory that will stay with you for a long time, and you may even burn through the knot you just made so carefully. Clip the end of the tag at an angle, but only once you are satisfied the knot has been formed and tightened correctly. Clipping properly leaves everything neat and smooth. Alternatively, when you have to wrap a splice, there are specific instructions in the information provided—be careful to follow the advice closely. Be sure to follow the advice as to how much tag end to leave hanging out of your finished knot—with stretchy line, and some knots, there must be allowance for the tag end to slip under tension.

One last piece of advice—if you find that you are regularly finishing your tag end with an overhand knot (it's okay once in a while), take a close look at how tightly you are making the wraps, because you may not be getting the wraps tight enough to trap the tag end properly. We know that the tag end is going to slip a little when we tie monofilament nylon, so allow for this small slippage when you trim the knot. Also check that you made the right number of wraps. Too many wraps cause too much friction and too few make for a knot guaranteed to come loose. The correct number of turns often depends on the thickness of the line.

You will find that you have to experiment sometimes to see just how much tension or pull is too much for your chosen line, and how much is not enough. This is where practice at home is a good thing. Take a piece of line and test it with your knot several times (ten tests should do it, and it's an easy number to remember) by pulling steadily on the line with gloved hands and then giving a quick final tug in several different directions, just like a fish would do—this assumes of course that you are testing some 2-pound or

6-pound line, not 150-pound line, which will need more strength than you can muster with your hands alone.

A more scientific test is to tie the knotted line to a pail that you gradually fill with water or sand. When the knot breaks, weigh the pail and then repeat the test several times to get an accurate assessment of knot strength. Run the same test with different knots to compare break strengths.

Yes, you will use up a lot of line in tests like this, but it's money and time well spent. A few dollars for a spool of line and one or two evenings spent bench testing is nothing compared to the cost of a trip to the Rogue River just to see the steelhead get away.

## What Not to Do

Using glue to finish a knot is useful, but be careful—cyanoacrylate or CA glue (commonly known as superglue) will melt some lines. Also remember that some CA glue requires the surfaces to be wet and some requires them to be dry and clean. Check the label.

Specific warnings are given where necessary in the text and on the packaging the glue comes in. When you use CA, do so with caution—it can be embarrassing to go to the emergency room with your fingers glued to your tackle-box.

In some cases two-part epoxy glue that is both waterproof and will not affect the line provides good results. Pliobond is a time-honored choice for particular applications. I like the stuff but some people cannot stand it—personal choice. Other cautions should be obvious: don't nick the line, use new, fresh line, don't burn the line, don't wrap the line around your unprotected hands to pull hard on it, and don't dump old or tangled line overboard.

# Chapter 2

# What You Need to Know About Line

*• Monofilament  • Braided Line  • Multifilament  • Fluorocarbon*
*• Wire  • Knots for Wire  • Figure Eight Knot  • Haywire*
*Twist*

You will be working with line every time you fish, so when you know what the characteristics of each kind of line are, you'll know why it works like it does, and you'll know also what it can and cannot do.

Fishing line was formerly made from linen, cotton, silk gut, or braided silk, and knots tended to stay put—life was simpler then. Fishing line is now made from a variety of plastics, including polyamide (nylon), polyester (Dacron), ultra-high molecular weight polyethylene (a monofilament also known as Spectra), polyvinylidenefluoride (PVDF also known as fluorocarbon), Dyneema (a multifilament gel-spun polyethylene or PE fiber), Vectran (a multifilament modified aromatic polyester melt extrusion liquid crystal polymer), and Kevlar (a multifilament aromatic polyamide or aramid fiber).

When selecting a monofilament line, you should first know whether or not you want least cost and greatest stretch (nylon), greatest flexibility and little stretch with maximal sensitivity (Dacron), or zero stretch, very high strength and higher cost (Kevlar).

One last item as a reminder—when you are handling *any* line that is rated over about 15- or 20-pound test, never try to break it or tighten your knots without gloves or pliers. You could end up in the ER with line embedded in your hands, and that would not only be painful, but also embarrassing.

# Monofilament

"Mono" means one and "filament" means thread, hence the name means a single thread. Monofilament is a name given to fishing line that is a single strand of extruded plastic made from a mixture of polymers (hence copolymer) or plastics that are drawn (pulled) or extruded (pushed) as a fine line through a computer-controlled spinneret. One of the first man-made monofilament lines was made of what was then a new substance, a polyamide known as nylon, developed by Dupont in 1938. Modern nylon monofilaments are often treated or combined with other materials to provide specific characteristics. Nylon is also available in different colors (blue, green, white or fluorescent, for night-time fishing) or clear. Clear is best when you want the line to be less visible to the fish.

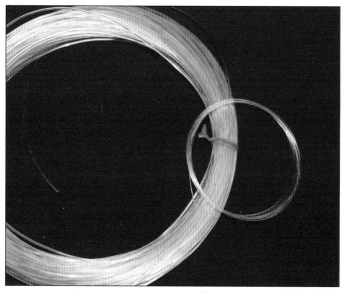

*Copolymer monofilament on the left (First String 135-pound-test leader by Izorline) and fluorocarbon leader (30-pound test Seaguar by Kureha) on the right—both are monofilaments but there is a huge difference in strength between them.*

Monofilaments can be tapered to produce knotless fly-fishing leaders. Nylon absorbs water (about 5 to 10 percent of its weight) and weakens when wet (about 20 percent strength loss), so this needs to be considered when choosing a break-strength to fish with.

Other plastics, like polyester, do not absorb water and do not lose strength when wet; Kevlar actually gains strength when wet, but is susceptible to ultra-violet light (sunlight), where it breaks down unless coated or covered. Based on cost, nylon is the most economical, polyester next, and Kevlar the most expensive fishing line.

Tying knots in monofilament presents some specific challenges, as we will see later.

Nylon line also has memory, so when you break out the reels from last year's fishing, you'll likely find that the line remembers the cozy way it was when put away, and you'll end up getting some hellacious snarls. If you don't use your gear all year round, you may find that after long storage nylon mono will coil up on itself, possibly making a snarl or tangle that cannot be undone. A word to the wise—check your line often and, if it looks dodgy, replace it.

## Braided Line

A braided line is a series of fibers that are woven together by machinery. The number of fibers in each yarn and the particular over-under weaving pattern is selected by the manufacturer to provide flexibility and durability. Most braided lines are highly abrasive, so watch your equipment for wear, and be aware that braids can easily cut your hands and fingers. Flexibility and abrasion resistance are normally not compatible—the more flexible a line, the less abrasion-resistant; and the more abrasion-resistant a line is, the less flexible it becomes. This quality is very important to consider when selecting a line for light tackle, which requires flexibility, or for bottom fishing, where abrasion resistance is important.

Braided line is made from the same materials that are used for monofilament. The different construction helps to make the tensile strength (the ability of the line to hold greater weights) higher for braided lines than for monofilament in a given diameter, but because of the added expense of the manufacturing, the line costs more than monofilament. The over-under pattern of braided line also includes a lot of air pockets and light-reflecting surfaces, which makes the braid more visible to the fish. This can be accommodated by adding a clear monofilament leader, which is less visible in the water.

As for the tendency that nylon line has to remember the neat coil it was in on your spool all last winter, forget that with polyester line and braided line—it will come off the spool easily, with no birdnesting or ballooning.

# Multifilament

A refinement on monofilament line is multifilament. These lines are highly sensitive because of their lack of stretch. They are formed with multiple strands of polyester filament tape, or Spectra, that is then fused together with a coating to provide a flexible and sensitive line. However, because of all the work in manufacturing and assembling such a line, which can be five to ten times stronger than steel of the same diameter, it also costs five times more than regular monofilament. Add to this the consideration that because it is so thin for its break strength, it takes more line to fill your reel, so a spoolful can be a substantial investment. Commonly, braided polyester line is used as backing to fill the reel, to which multifilament is attached as the working line, thus reducing the need for a lot of expensive line that rarely gets used.

# Fluorocarbon

Fluorocarbon line, also known as PVDF, deserves attention, because it is popular with anglers who want strength and the ability for the line to disappear in water. Fluoro lines virtually and visually disappear in water (you and the fish cannot see them) and are stronger than mono for a given diameter. They do not absorb water and neither lose nor gain strength when wet. Fluorocarbon lines are also of monofilament construction, and while the material is somewhat stiffer than nylon, the knotting characteristics are essentially identical.

# Wire

### Single Strand

- **Monel:** Monel is a single strand wire that is highly resistant to corrosion, making it suitable for a salt-water environment. It is mostly used for wire-line trolling.
- **Stainless:** Single-strand stainless steel comes in a variety of types—the more corrosion-resistant is type 316, which is okay to use in the marine environment, as it resists the pitting and corrosion that attack lesser quality stainless steels. This single strand wire is available in silver and coffee-colored, and is standard as leader material when both casting and trolling for toothy species.
- **Multi-strand Cable:** Multi-strand stainless cable comes in all sizes, from light enough to be used in casting, to heavy "aircraft cable" for maximum strength in big-game fishing.

In the lighter weights it is available both coated and uncoated. Coated cable is easier to handle, but the coating is not as durable as the cable, and, after a few toothy catches, may need to be replaced. The advantage to multi-strand cable leaders over single strand in casting weights is that multi-strand is more flexible, and transmits better action to the lure than single strand. Big game cable, in heavier strengths, provides excellent flexibility for trolling lures and enough strength to handle the biggest fish that swim. But the extreme strength combined with flexibility creates an ever-present danger. Death or dismemberment is a real threat when handling strong fish on a heavy cable leader. It is for the expert and experienced only. Even in the lightest weights, multi-strand cable requires special knots or crimping.

### Crimping

Multi-strand cable, braided, line, and heavy mono can all be crimped, but require special tools and sleeves sized to the size of the line you intend to crimp. Care and skill must be employed to properly crimp for maximum strength. Big-game cable is not easy to damage, but you must be certain not to cut any of the fine wire strands. Braided line can be crimped to form a loop or attachment, but it may be better to try to learn how to splice the line instead.

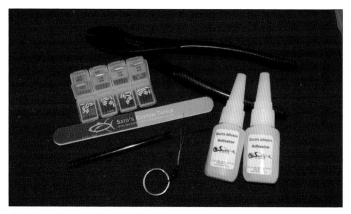

*Crimping: An outfit for crimping Spectra, stainless wire, or heavy monofila-
ment includes sleeves, crimping tool, adhesives, and specialized tools
for working with particular lines. The small loop in the lower left helps
with threading braided line. The purple tube is a splicing tool. Use the polish-
ing paper to smooth the end of monofilament when joining it to braided line.*

Heavy monofilament will readily accept crimping, but be careful
not to pinch part of the line in the crimp itself. Small nicks in the
line can compromise the break strength.

## Knots for Wire

Fastening wire to fishing line or to a hook eye is pretty straightforward. There are a couple of connections that work very well, and
not much else that does. So we'll dispense with knots for wire right
off the bat and get them out of the way.

The most common knot for fastening light multi-strand cable,
both coated and uncoated, to a hook eye is the Figure Eight Knot.

## Figure Eight Knot

Single-strand stainless wire is fastened to a hook of lure with a
loop, using the Haywire Twist. The other end can be fastened to
small swivel with the same twist, or attached to the fishing line with
an Albright knot.

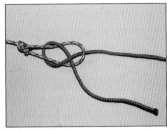

*Tied in wire at left. The knot formation, tied with easier-to-see cord, is in the picture on the right. Hold the wire with pliers or very strong fingers. Note the loop on the sinker is a swivel fitting and you are looking at it edge-on.*

*This knot should be tightened by pulling on both the standing part and the tag end at the same time. Nylon coating on the wire will melt if heated gently with a match, helping it to stay in place. Again, see the structure on the right, in heavy cord.*

## Haywire Twist

The principle of the Haywire Twist is simple, but requires practice. It's essential to form both the initial wide twist and the final tight wraps for this knot to work. In the first section both strands should be twisted together; in the finishing wraps, the tag end is wrapped closely around the standing part of the wire.

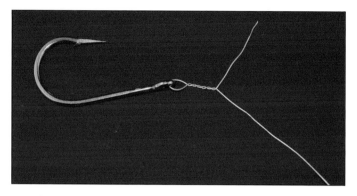

1 Set the two strands at right angles to each other and twist *both* together.

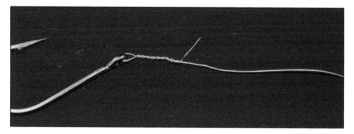

2 Keeping the standing part straight, bend the tag end to wrap tightly around the standing part. You may need five or six turns. Once the tight wraps are complete, bend the tag end at a right angle to form a little crank (not shown) then rotate this to snap off the tag close to the wraps. This eliminates any sharp end that can snag and cut. This wrap must be broken off closely to the wraps. It is impossible to clip it closely enough to make a smooth end, but breaking it off does the job.

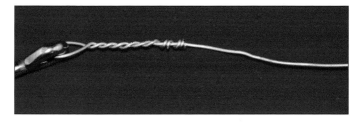

3 The finished twist.

# Chapter 3

## Knots You Need to Know

• *Arbor Knot* • *Australian Braid* • *Bimini Twist*
• *Crawford Knot* • *Improved Clinch Knot* • *Jansik Special*
• *Japanese Fisherman's Knot* • *Offshore Swivel Knot*
• *Orvis Knot* • *Overhand Knot* • *Palomar Knot* • *Snelling*
• *Trilene Knot*

All anglers have a few special knots for general situations and general use. This list of about a dozen knots in alphabetical order is one that I find is useful to remember and practice whenever I get a moment to twist a piece of line. If you can remember and practice these, you'll be better at remembering and using the other knots in the book. A word to the wise here: You will see many books referring to the strength of the knot being as much as a claimed 200 percent of the strength of the line. This is clearly nonsense, unless you know what they are talking about. What they are really claiming is that the knot does not break until 200 percent (or whatever number they give you) of the manufacturer's stated breaking strength of the line. This number is found by breaking dozens or perhaps even hundreds of samples of line in a testing machine, under rigorous conditions of quality control in a laboratory. All the breaking strengths are then added up and divided by the number of tests to provide an average number for the break strength. As with many things in the scientific world, the average is just a number—it is not a guarantee. A clever mathematics teacher once told me that, if I stand with one foot on the stove and the other foot in the refrigerator, on average I would be comfortable. Clearly these extremes are unusual, but they are still correct when talking about an average—you need to know how many tests were done, what the spread of numbers (highest to lowest) was and if the line was all from the same production batch.

It is not unusual to have strength tests that differ widely from each other—the mathematical term for this is standard deviation. This just means that some strengths are higher and some are lower than the average. Taken overall, the average strength of a piece of line can be beaten by (or not do as well as) any other piece of the same line, sometimes even from the same batch. So, when a knot is claimed to perform at 200 percent of the breaking strength (which is implying that the knot makes the line stronger) it just means that several people got lucky once or twice and tested the knot using line that was performing better than the manufacturer's tests had shown to be the average strength, or that the strength number was under-stated. Knots will almost make a line weaker, though in the case of some knots, such as the Bimini Twist, the line will break before the knot, if it is tied properly. The point at which the line will break is almost always at the point where it enters the knot, because this is where it is first bent out of shape by the knot, inducing tension on one side of the line and compression on the other. Sometimes a knot will break at a different point within the line and sometimes, as mentioned above, the line will break outside the knot altogether. These are normal variances and may even be expected. It does not mean that a knot improves the strength of the line. You will also occasionally have a line break where there was a defect in the line, which, with modern manufacturing methods, happens a lot less frequently than with the older types of line. Enough of the physics already—let's get on with the knots.

## Arbor Knot

Before you can start fishing, you'll need this knot to secure the line to your reel. When tying extra-slippery, non-stretch lines to the arbor, put a piece of tape around the arbor first, so knotted line has something to bite into. Otherwise the entire spoolful is likely to rotate around the arbor under pressure. The Arbor Knot uses an overhand knot on the standing part of your line, backed up by another overhand knot like this:

1 Wrap line around your spool in a clockwise direction.

2 Tie an overhand knot around the standing part and slip the tag end through it.

3 Tie an overhand in the tag end and pull it tight.

4 Slide the completed knot down to fit snugly onto your arbor.

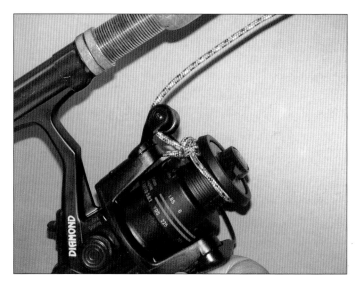

5 Put the spool back on the reel and start taking up line.

## Australian Braid

Use this knot to form a double line or as a substitute for a Bimini Twist. This knot passes through the rod guides without catching. This is a braid or plait, formed with the end of the line that leaves a loop at the end. Be sure to braid the line for the distance recommended or you will find there is some considerable slippage—it is probably better to make it before you go, when your hands are more supple and you can manage the line more easily. If you are going to make this in nylon, be sure to practice first using a thicker piece of braid in Dacron so that your hands remember how to make it.

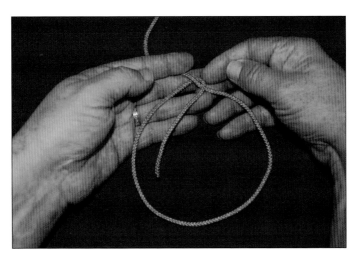

1 Form a loop around the standing part.

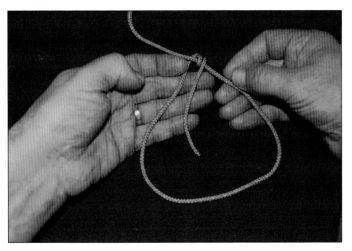

2 Make a complete round turn about the standing part.

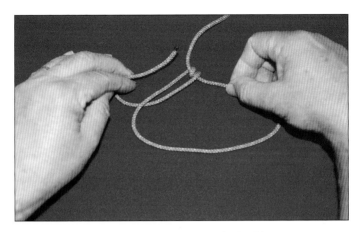

3 Separate the three parts as shown for braiding.

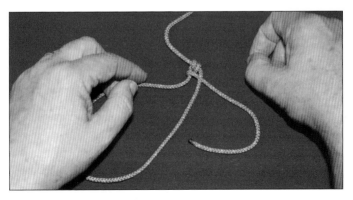

4 Start braiding, right over left, left over right, passing each stand into the center each time.

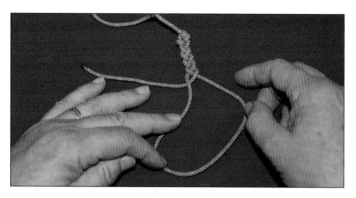

5 Braid completed after four wraps over from the right for nylon, two more for fluorocarbon.

6 Make two turns completely around the two legs of the loop.

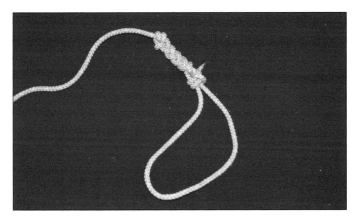

7 Tuck the tag end back through the braiding just above where you made the turns around both legs, and pull everything gently but firmly together.

## Bimini Twist

When you want to maintain your line at 100 percent of its rated break strength, the Bimini Twist is the knot to choose. When this knot is completed, the loop that results provides two strands that are used together, as if they were a single piece, when tying to another line or to a hook eye. Often the loop is clipped and the two strands are twisted together, and this twist is then used as a single line to make the next connection.

The trick to this knot is controlling the tension properly as the knot is formed. Practice this knot before setting out—there's nothing quite like the frustration of trying to tie a BT when the wind is blowing, and the boat is rocking.

As an alternative to this knot for maintaining maximum strength, try the Japanese Fisherman's Knot or the Australian Braid.

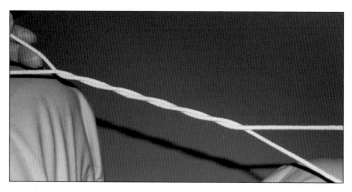

1 Make a loop that is nearly twice as long as you need it and twist the loop 20 times around with your hand, while holding the tag end and the standing part together.

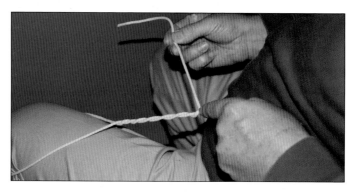

2 Place the loop around your foot and pull it up over your knee, then pull on both ends to twist the lines together and put the twist under tension.

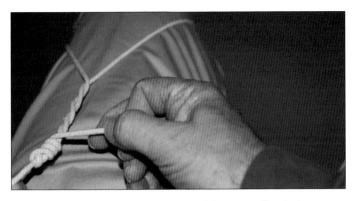

3 This step reverses the direction of the tag, rolling it down over the twist, heading back toward the loop. Release the tension on the tag end slightly and feed the tag around the twists as they spin. At this point you can assist the rollover by straightening your leg to help the twisted portion spin, as you feed the tag smoothly down over the twists.

4 Then hold the last of the wraps firmly with your left hand while you tie a half hitch around one leg of the loop.

5 Then tie another half hitch around the other leg of the loop. At this point the knot should be stable.

6 Now make a two-or three-wrap half hitch around both legs of the loop.

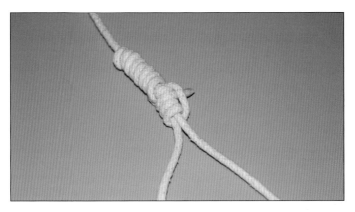

7 Pull the tag end tightly to snug up the finishing half hitches. Trim the excess, leaving a short tag so the half hitches do not work loose.

## Crawford Knot

The Crawford Knot is a secure knot to use with a monofilament or Spectra leader, because the wraps develop the inherent strength you are looking for. It is a jamming wrap, relying on the tag end jammed into the space between the wraps and the eye on your hook. It can be difficult to fetch up securely unless lubricated well, but is a good knot to remember for a secure tie.

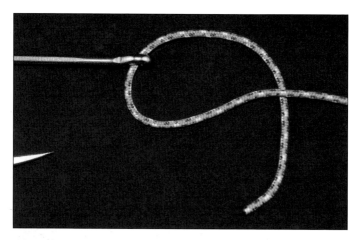

1 Pass the line clockwise through the eye and under the standing part.

2 Wrap over both parts of the loop you just made, to the left, and tuck the tag end under both parts.

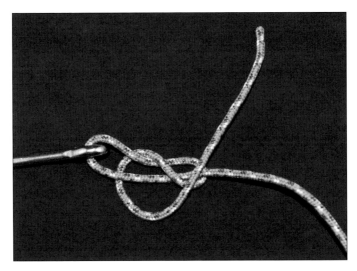

3 Bring the tag end over the two legs of the loop, this time to the right.

4 Tuck the tag end, from underneath, into the top loop.

5 Tuck the end back through the loop you first made by the eye.

6 Fair the knot and draw it down tight to the hook, lure, or sinker.

## Improved Clinch Knot

This variation on the standard Clinch Knot has a small improvement in the last step, which makes it more secure in mono because of that extra pinch point.

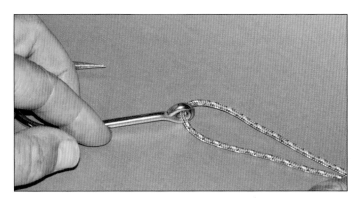

1 Pass the standing part through the eye, clockwise.

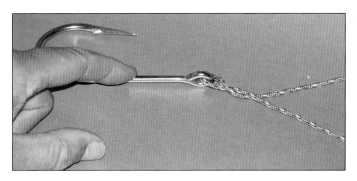

2 Form a loop over the standing part.

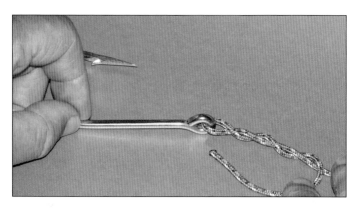

3 Make at least three more turns over the standing part, six for slippery line.

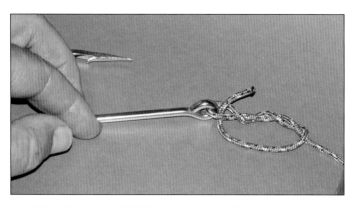

4 Pass the tag end UP through the loop by the eye.

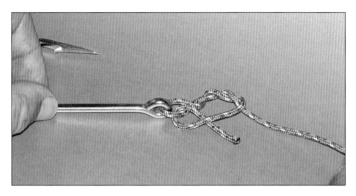

5 Pass the tag end DOWN through the tag end's own loop.

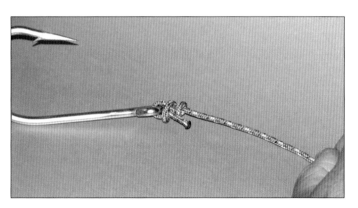

6 Gradually work the wetted turns together, pulling the stand-ing part, and then trim the tag end.

## Jansik Special

This is a high-strength knot, especially favored by muskie fisher-men. Its strength comes from the number of turns the line makes through the hook-eye. Those turns and their finishing wraps are important to spreading the load on the line, so don't skimp on them just because they are hard to make.

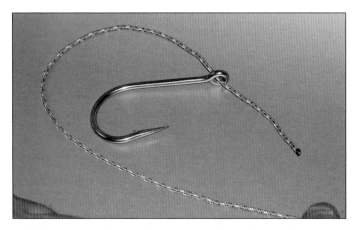

1 Make a loop through the eye, in a clockwise direction.

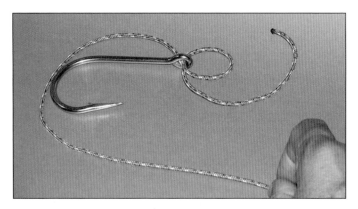

2 Bring the tag end through the eye again.

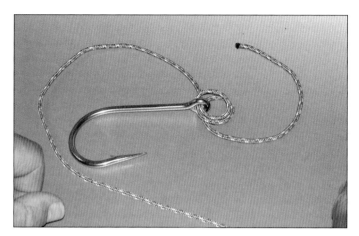

3 Bring the tag end through the eye a third time.

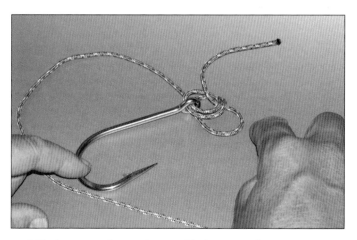

4 Start to wrap the two loops with the tag end.

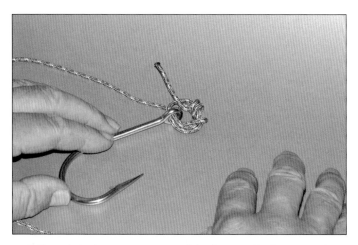

5 Complete three wraps around the loops with the tag end.

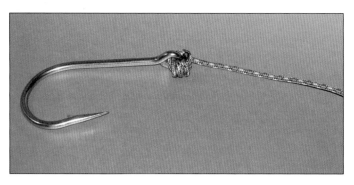

6 Fair the knot by pulling on the standing part, gradually working the two loops both through the eye until they are firm, and tightly holding the wraps from Step 5.

## Japanese Fisherman's Knot

This knot has its origins in the ancient art of hand lining, and beats all when it comes to sheer strength. The strength comes from the number of wraps, which spread the load along the line instead of concentrating it at one point.

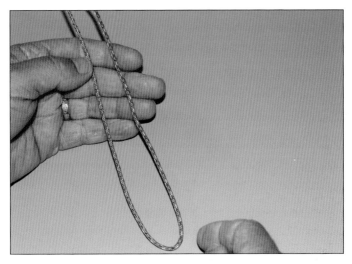

1 Make a bight with one end of the line. Now is the time to put a hook or lure on the bight if this is to be an attachment knot.

2 Twist the loop about five or six turns, depending on the line used to make the knot.

3 Start wrapping back over the twist you made.

4 Continue wrapping down over the previous turns until you reach the original loop.

5 Make a half hitch around both legs of the loop, and stick the tag end through the middle of the loop.

6 Then take the tag end around the right-hand leg as shown here and tie a half hitch around that leg only.

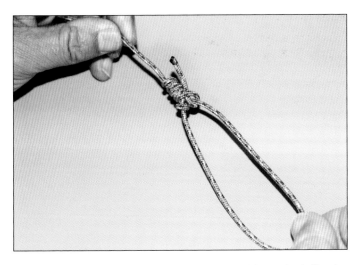

7 Finish off by pulling everything fair and tight, to look like the photograph.

# Offshore Swivel Knot

Fishing offshore requires that you use something really hardy and capable of taking a beating. A swivel attached to your double-line leader with this knot will stick like glue and never let go. It needs some care in tightening, but is well worth the effort to make it right. It gets its power from the fact that it has so many twists, from an old knot known as a Cat's-paw, in which each of the twists bears against the next twist, sharing the load throughout the hitch, a bit like a zipper, but without being able to unzip. To untie it, you simply have to wiggle the knot open a little and then reverse the direction of tying it.

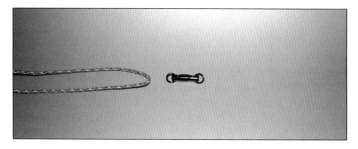

1 Make a loop in the end of the leader or use a spliced loop if using Dacron braid.

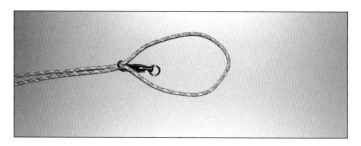

2 Pass the loop through the swivel ring.

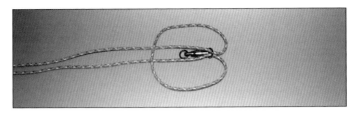

3 Flip the loop back over itself to the left, leaving the swivel on the right.

4 Turn the swivel back over itself to the right.

5 Repeat Stage 4 five more times (six in all).

6 Wet the knot thoroughly and draw the twisted loops slowly together, rolling the twists toward the swivel as you go.

## Orvis Knot

The Orvis Company ran a contest to find the best line-to-hook knot. This knot, by Larry Becker of Waskom, Texas, was the winner. It is simple in construction, secure because it does not let go, and strong enough to warrant winning the contest. Orvis judges recognized it as a winner because of the ease with which it can be remembered and tied. The more I have looked at and used the Orvis knot, the more I am convinced that it is an extension of the Timber Hitch, a very useful and secure knot used in old square-rigged ships and on small day-sailor ships to attach a reefing line. Combine those attributes with the base figure eight around the standing part of your line and it is small wonder it was declared the winner. It is in any case a very secure knot.

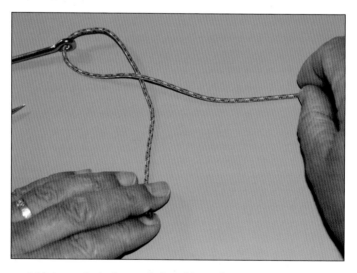

1 Make a clockwise underhand loop through the hook or lure eye.

2 Bring the tag end over the standing part of the line to make a figure eight.

3 Start to make what appears to be a second figure eight, but keep wrapping the tag end around that arm of the first eight, one more time.

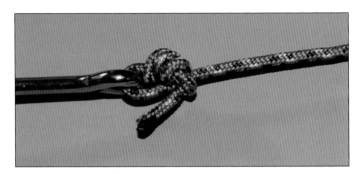

4 Now fair up the knot by tightening the wraps around the second eight and then pulling the first eight tighter.

## Overhand Knot

Here is an interesting fact: did you know that two overhand knots tied in the same direction make a granny knot, or that two overhand knots tied first to the left and then to the right make a square knot? The overhand makes a helpful stopper knot—if you don't mind that it is usually permanent. It is also the basis for many of the other knots in this book, is a knot that can be tied by the wind, and may have been one of the first knots ever tied by primitive man. Shown are two distinct types of overhand knot, one left-handed and one right-handed. Both are correct—just be sure to use the same type each time.

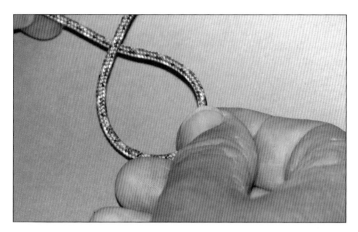

1 (RH Overhand) Bring the tag end around over the standing part in a clockwise direction.

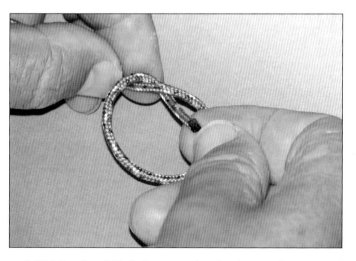

2 (RH Overhand) Tuck the tag end under the standing part and then through the loop you have formed.

3 (RH Overhand) The completed knot, not yet faired up; leave the tag end sticking out about 1/4-inch after fairing the knot.

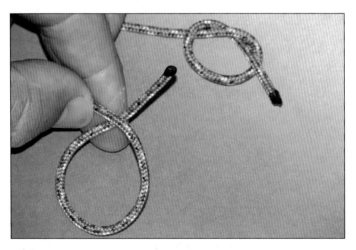

4 (LH Overhand) Bring the tag end around under the standing part, clockwise.

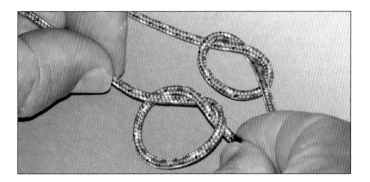

5 (LH Overhand) Seen here below the RH Overhand; tuck the tag end down into the loop and pull through from underneath.

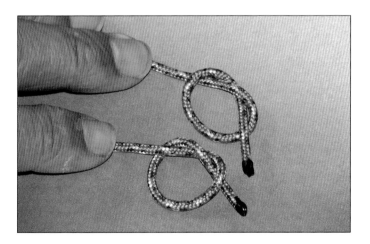

6 Here are the RH Overhand and the LH Overhand together before fairing.

## Palomar Knot

If you are looking for a knot to use reliably with braid line, this is it. The Palomar is easily tied, easily remembered and is very useful as a terminal knot for your gear. It can be tied using a loop (bight) or with a doubled line—either way, it will not come loose. A word to the wise—if you are tying a double or triple hook, don't use this knot, as the hooks are likely to get tangled in the loop at some point during the tying.

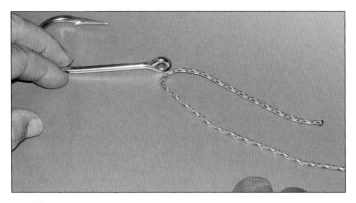

1 Bring a loop to the eye of the hook.

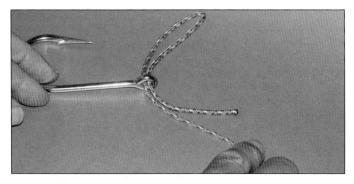

2 Pass the loop through the eye.

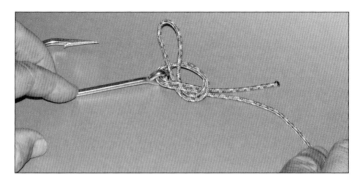

3 Make an overhand knot with the loop.

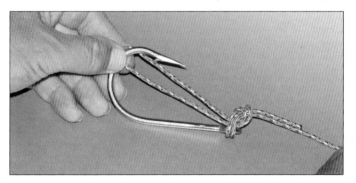

4 Pass the loop over the hook to pass behind the shank.

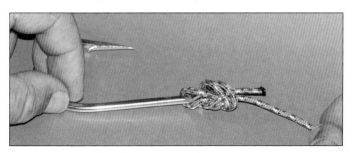

5 Fair the knot by pulling the overhand knot tight around the shank and then up over.

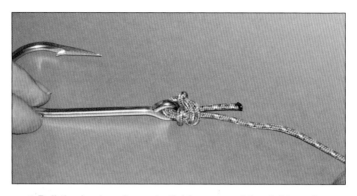

6 Pull the knot and eye, to tighten around the tightened over-hand loop knot, then trim away the tag end.

## Snelling

Snelling is a word that was first used in print in the U.S. in 1893, when reference was made in Volume XXII of the February issue of the sporting magazine *Outing* to "well made, securely wrapped, double-snelled Aberdeen bend hooks." The origin of the word in Old English means quick or sharp, so I would guess that the name was given on account of the finished appearance of the hook shank being "sharp" when attached like this.

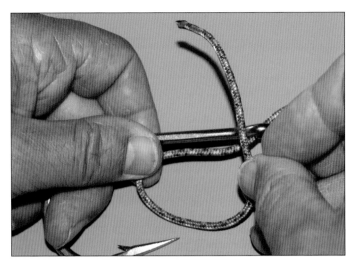

1 Pass the line through the hook eye and along the shank, then return, forming an overhand counterclockwise loop below the shank.

2 Make wraps around the shank and the upper part of the loop, until you have from four to seven wraps or more, depending on your line.

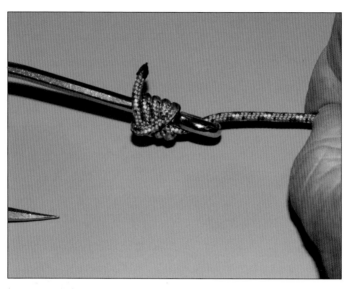

3 Fair up the knot by rolling it around the shank with your fingers, cutting away the tag end when you are satisfied the wraps are tight enough. Use a hook with a bent eye, NOT the type shown here.

## Trilene Knot

Used for tying monofilament to swivels, snaps, lures, hooks, and sinkers, this is a versatile knot and easily tied and remembered. Like the Jansik, the round turns ensure that it does not let go. The structure of the first and last part of this knot is like the start of the Fisherman's Bend, a useful knot for attaching an anchor. With the final tuck under the last pass into the turns, there is an improvement in security.

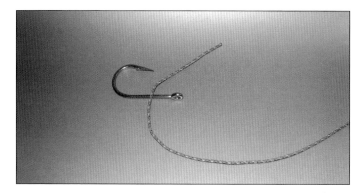

1 Take the tag end of your line.

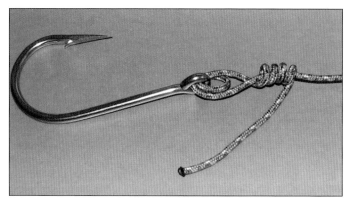

2 And pass it through the eye twice to form a round turn.

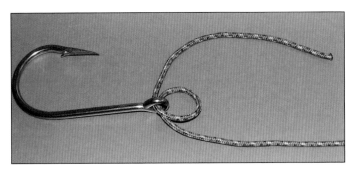

3 Then take the tag end around the standing part about four or five times for braided or superline, tucking it up into the round turn you made through the eye. Make six turns if you are using nylon or seven turns if using fluorocarbon.

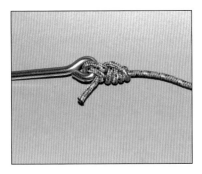

4 Wet the knot, pull tight, and trim the tag end, but not too close.

# Chapter 4

## Line to Line Knots—Making Ends Meet

· *Albright Knot with a Lock* · *Bending Monel to Braid*
· *Blood Knot (Simple)* · *Improved Blood Knot* · *Huffnagle Knot* · *Surgeon's Knot*

"Many's the time and oft," as the poet Dibdin once said, and he may well have been commenting on the need to connect one type or thickness of line to another, such as attaching a leader to the fishing line, replacing the fine tippet on a fly leader, or connecting backing to the main line. These knots can be useful when lines must be joined together.

## Albright Knot with a Lock

The Albright Knot has a great history, and it's a standby for tying light mono to heavier lines and leaders like heavy mono, single-strand wire, or nylon-coated wire. It is trim enough to pass through the rod guides smoothly. The lock on this one brings a certain peace of mind to knowing that the tag end is not going to back out of the knot during a fight. It is sometimes known as the Key Loop with a Lock and the Key Knot Splice with a Lock.

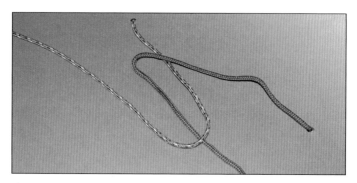

1 Loop each line through the other (solid blue is the lighter line; light blue is the heavier line or wire).

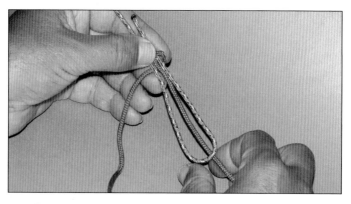

2 Start making turns around the legs of the loop, winding the lighter line back down the loop, over itself.

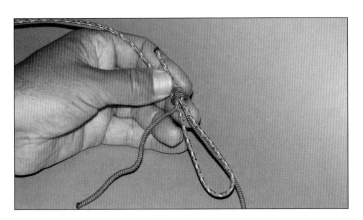

3 Continue wrapping . . .

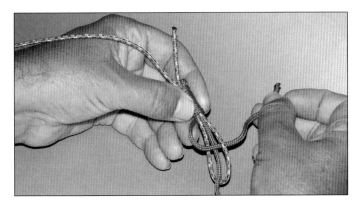

4 . . . until you have six turns, then tuck the tag end through the loop.

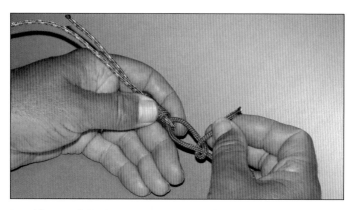

5 Then pull the loop through the wraps to capture the tag end. Make turns with the tag end around its own standing part and tuck it through the loop that has formed.

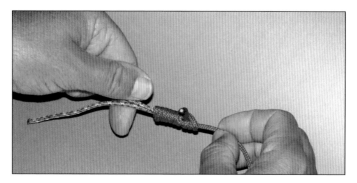

6 Pull hard on the tag end to make the turns snug against the loop end.

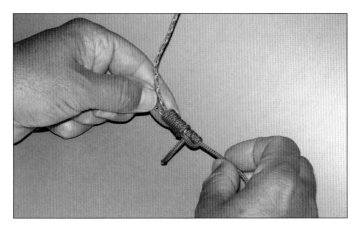

7 Here is what it looks like from the other side.

## Bending Monel to Braid

*Bending* is the term used when you tie one line to another line. Here, you almost could be forgiven for thinking that bending means literally bending the Monel wire so as to attach it to the braided line. So, why attach braided to Monel? Monel helps to get a trolling lure deep where you need it, but is seldom used to fill the spool. A hundred feet of Monel over a spool of braided Dacron is a common configuration for deep trolling, when only as much wire is used as is needed to gain the required depth.

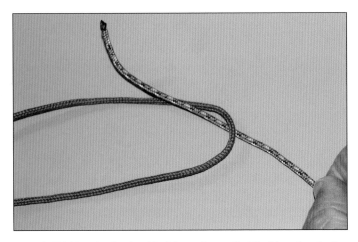

1 Solid blue is the braided line; the red/white/blue line is the Monel. Bring the Monel up through a bight in the line.

2 Wrap the Monel around the line, keeping the line straight and tight while you make the wraps.

3 Overwrap the Monel around itself past the end of the braided bight.

4 Make a Haywire Twist in the wire to finish off, pulling the wire down tight against the braided bight.

5 Be sure to tightly wrap the last end of the wire against itself to make sure it does not snag. Use Pliobond if necessary to hold everything in place and create a smooth, snag-free profile to bend.

## Blood Knot (Simple)

The simple Blood Knot is an elegant knot for joining lines of the same or similar diameter. Be sure to take the number of turns suggested, or you may find that the knot slips and comes apart. Lighter lines require more turns than heavier lines.

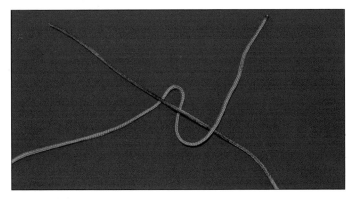

1 Lay the two lines together and overlapped about six inches.

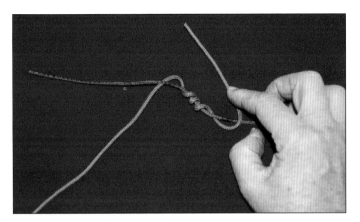

2 Pinch one line under the other (here the blue is pinched under) with its tag to the right and wrap it around the other standing part about four to six times.

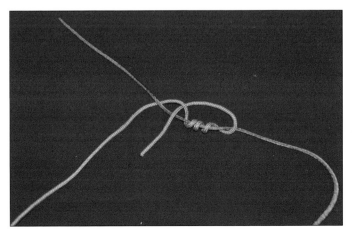

3 Tuck the tag end down between the two lines.

4 Repeat this with the other tag end, being sure to wrap in the opposite direction.

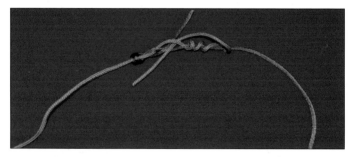

5 Tuck the second tag end through the wraps in the opposite direction of the first.

6 Form the loose knot up evenly and lubricate it with water or saliva, then pull steadily and firmly on both standing ends until the knot is formed. Tighten this knot with one steady pull. It is difficult or impossible to form properly unless it is tightened in one smooth operation.

## Complex Blood Knot

I call this one the Complex Blood Knot because it takes a little more practice than the simple blood knot and because it is not really a Blood Knot; it only vaguely resembles it. It is used only when you want to attach a light line to a heavier one—the Blood Knot will not do it so easily, and this one is easy to remember. Don't bother trying to use it to tie two same-size lines together—it will just make for a bulky knot. The Complex Blood Knot is used to help make sure that the light line is not overstressed and that, where the heavier line bends back on itself, it does not cut the lighter line—hence the good reason for doubling the lighter line. One more thing to add to the complexity; you could try leaving a dropper loop for a second hook instead of cutting away the light line loop where it passes through the center of the wraps. That way you get a two-for-one knot.

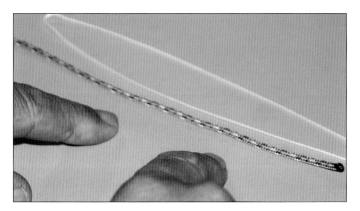

1 Make a bight in both lines.

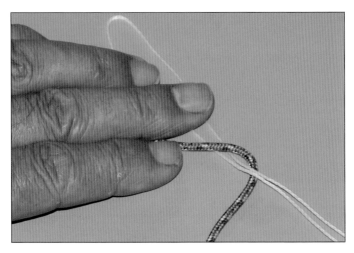

2 Start wrapping the heavier line around the lighter line.

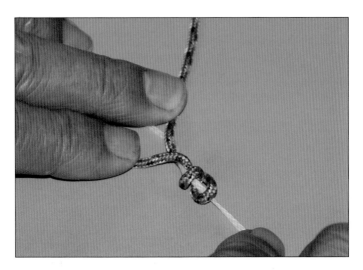

3 Bring the third or fourth (last) wrap between itself and the lighter line. This forms one side of the knot.

4 Now take the bight of leader and wrap it around the main line.

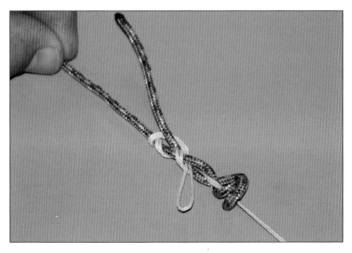

5 Tuck it over itself and down into the space where the tag of the main line sits. Be sure to tuck it OVER the main line tag as shown here.

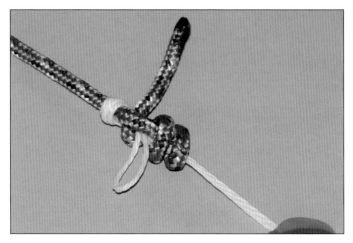

6 Draw the two lines apart, gradually rolling the leader bight tighter around the main line. If you need a loop at this point for a second leader, keep the leader bight, otherwise cut away the leader bight and the tag end of the main line to create a free-running knot. Coat with Pliobond if needed.

## Huffnagle Knot

As with most knots where you want to join a light line to a heavy line, you have to prepare the light line first. Let's say that you are looking to connect a fly leader tippet to a good strong line, such as 80-pound test, or heavier. First, make a Bimini Twist in your light line. This double strand will be used to tie the knot to the heavier material. You will need to lubricate this knot to snug it down, and pliers to effectively tighten it.

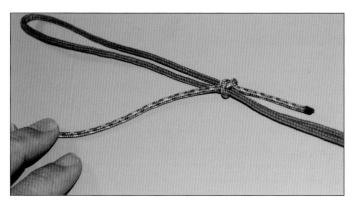

1 With the heavier material, tie an overhand knot around the doubled strand of the leader.

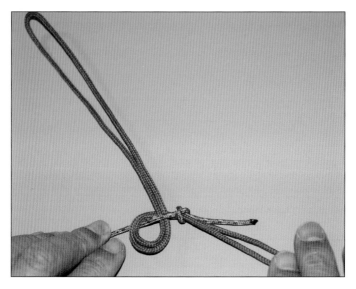

2 Start wrapping the leader bight around the standing part of your main line, behind the overhand knot.

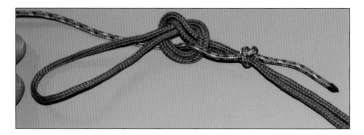

3 Tie an overhand around your main line using the bight of the leader and snug it down hard against the overhand already in your main line.

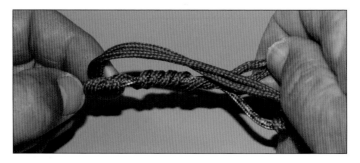

4 Wrap the leader bight several times (four or five) around the main line, being sure not to trap the bight under your wraps.

5 Pull the bight through and snug the wraps down against the leader's own overhand knot.

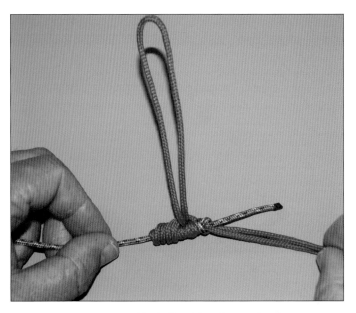

6 The tag ends should look like this prior to trimming.

7 If you used a Bimini Twist to get your initial loop, fair the knot to get the BT's wraps down to the overhand knot. Otherwise, tuck the tag end of the bight under a half hitch to finish. Trim away both tag ends and coat with Pliobond.

## Surgeon's Knot

This is an extension of the simple overhand knot that uses an extra tuck through the knot to develop, in the same way the Cat's Paw does, more friction by adding an extra twist. It is called the Surgeon's Knot as it is used in surgery to provide a better grip on the ligature to bring wound edges together.

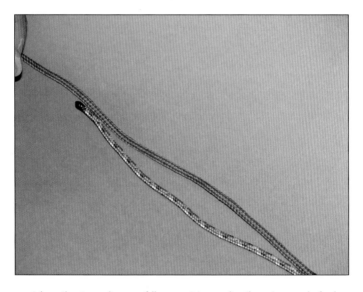

1 Lay the two pieces of line next to each other, tag ends facing away from each other.

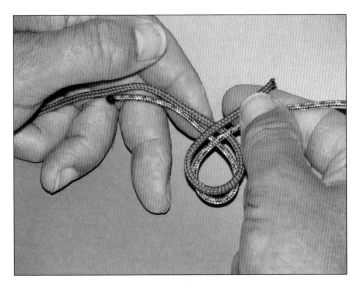

2 Make an overhand loop with both lines.

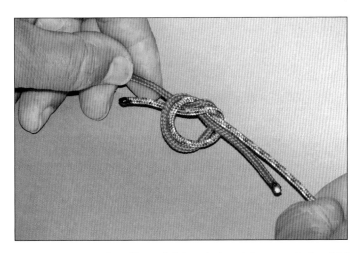

3 Make an overhand knot, left-handed or right, your choice (RH shown).

4 Double the overhand knot by adding another turn around the knot.

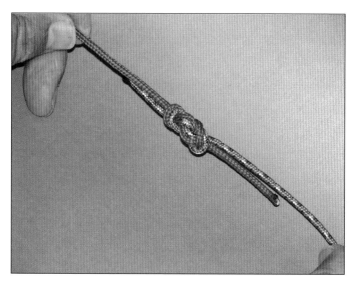

5 Fair the knot tightly, being sure to roll both parts toward each other—a little lubrication would help here.

# Chapter 5

# Getting Hooked with Loops

*· Interlocking Loops  · Duncan Loop  · Egg Loop (aka Salmon Egg Loop)  · Homer Rhode Loop  · Mono Loop (non-slip)  · Perfection Loop (aka Angler's Loop) · Surgeon's Loop  · Splicing a Loop in Dacron*

Attaching a line directly to the hook involves passing the end of the line through the eye of the hook. Nothing very complicated or difficult about that, so why the need to know about putting a loop through the hook instead? One reason is that a loop spreads the load of the line over the eye of the hook (you are using twice as much line with a loop as you do with a single line), which lowers the load on the individual strands of line. The second, and probably equally important reason is security. You want your knot to stay in place on the eye of the hook. Loops develop greater security than regular knots and hitches. Try these few select loop-to-hook knots and hitches and see if they don't improve the security of your hooks.

## Interlocking Loops

When you attach one loop to another, you will need access to one end of one of the lines to which the loop is attached. Don't try to pass a fully loaded reel and rod through a leader loop.

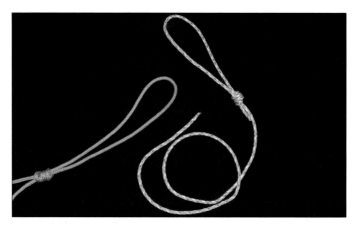

1 Two loops already made—use your favorites.

2 Insert the leader loop into the main line loop.

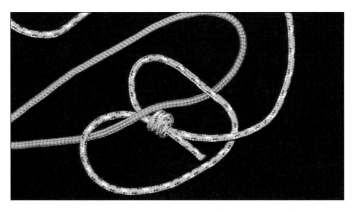

3 Take the other end of the leader and insert it through its own loop only.

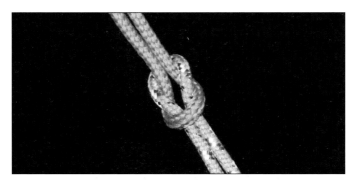

4 Pull both loops away from each other and they should flip to look like this.

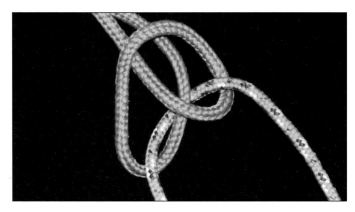

5 This is not quite perfect, but it will probably slip into place with pressure.

6 This configuration is weak and will cut through itself.

# Duncan Loop

Alongside the Homer Rhode Loop and the non-slip Mono Loop knot, the Duncan Loop is a favorite among anglers for forming a strong loop that allows the hook or lure to swing freely. Under pressure, when fighting a fish, the loop will close, giving you a tighter and more secure knot. Be sure you make the wraps tightly.

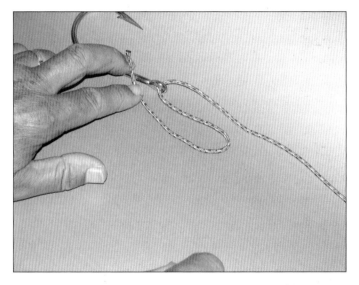

1 Pass the tag end through the eye and make an S-shape.

2 Wrap only one side of the S-shape with the tag end.

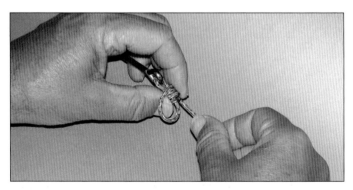

3 Continue wrapping until you have at least three turns.

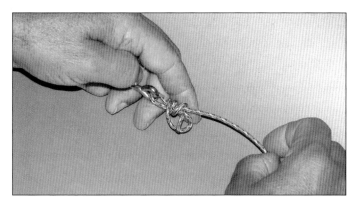

4 Pass the tag end through the loop you have formed. Adjust the loop to proper size by sliding the knot on the standing line, then tighten it in place by pulling on the tag end.

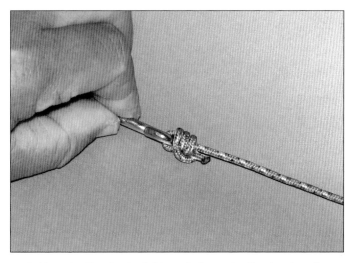

5 Here is the knot, tightened down to the hook—after a strike.

# Egg Loop (aka Salmon Egg Loop)

Trying to get salmon eggs to stay in place can be a major headache unless you try this little trick. This handy device will provide you with a good solid seating and a built-in trap to keep things where you want them—on the hook.

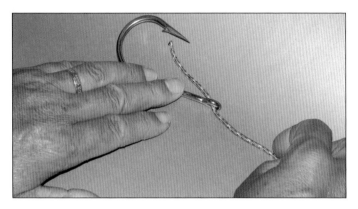

1 Pass the tag end through the eye.

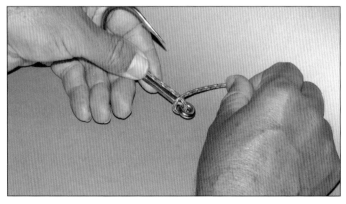

2 Lay the tag end along the shank and make turns of the standing part around tag end and shank.

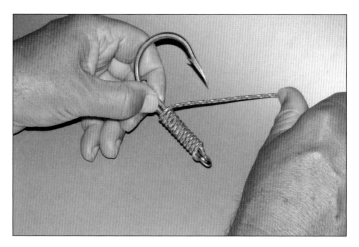

3 Keep making turns until you have at least seven turns.

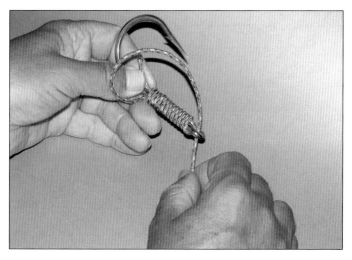

4 Make a loop with the standing part and pass the standing end through the eye, but keep it loose.

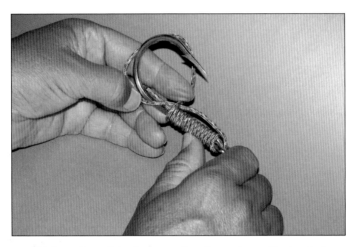

5 Make twists of the loop you just formed over the hook, trapping the tag end with your new wraps.

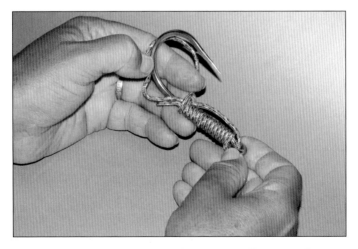

6 After three twists and wraps, stop and pull the standing part to tighten the wraps onto the tag end.

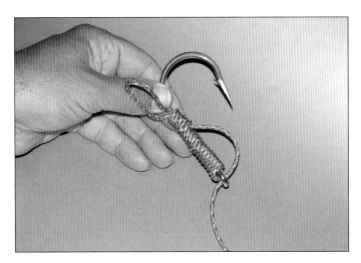

7 Tighten the standing part almost down onto the shank.

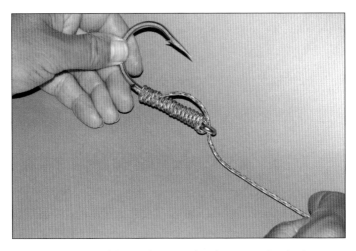

8 Now your hook is ready to receive the roe under the loop you created—the tension on your line will handily hold the eggs in place.

## Homer Rhode Loop

This always makes me think about Homer Simpson, although of course he has nothing to do with Homer Rhode, the guide in the Florida Keys for whom the knot was named. This knot is also sometimes known as the Flemish Loop or the Loop Knot, for those who are not aware of Homer Rhode. The knot enables the lure to swing freely and it can be tied with mono or braided line, even plastic-coated wire if need be. Be sure to use pliers to make the turns tight.

1 Tie an overhand knot in the standing part and pass the tag end through the eye.

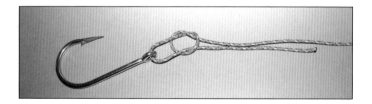

2 Pass the tag end through the loop of the overhand knot.

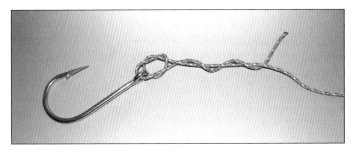

3 Make three or more turns of the tag end around the standing part, depending on the type of line (the slipperier, the more turns).

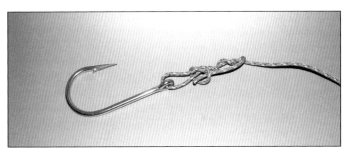

4 Pass the tag end back through the overhand loop.

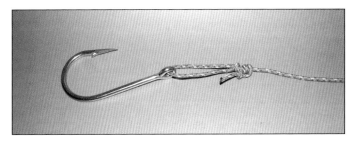

5 Tighten the turns and pull the tag end to bring the wraps together, then pull the standing part to tighten the knot.

## Mono Loop (non-slip)

Here is the third great stand-by. It is non-slip because of the wraps, so in light line or slipperier line, use more wraps.

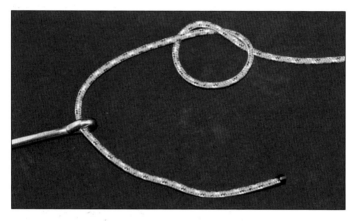

1 First, make an overhand knot, but don't pull it tight.

2 Pass the tag end through the eye of the hook and pass the tag back through the overhand knot the same way it exited the knot

3 Wrap the tag end around the standing part three to five times, depending on what line you are using.

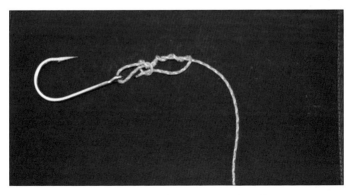

4 Bring the tag end back through the overhand.

5 Fair up the knot and cut away the tag end as needed.

# Perfection Loop (aka Angler's Loop)

This loop knot allows the slipperiest line, or even bungee cord, to be tied so that it will not slip.

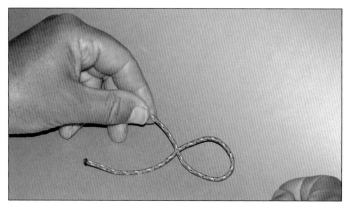

1 Form a first counterclockwise underhand loop.

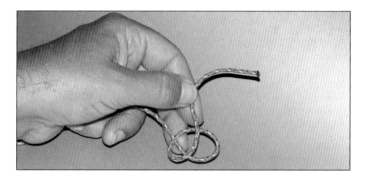

2 Continue to wind the tag end counterclockwise over the standing part to make the second loop.

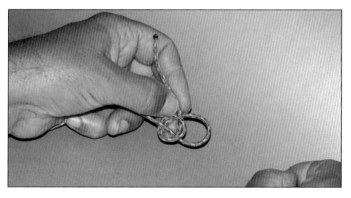

3 Position the tag end between the two loops and pull the top loop down through the lower loop . . .

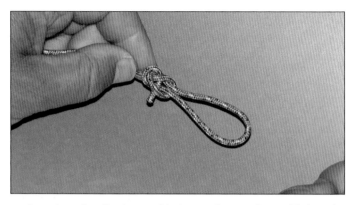

4 . . . trapping the tag end between the two loops. Tighten by pulling on the loop.

## Surgeon's Loop

Like the Surgeon's Knot, the Surgeon's Loop will not slip in the slickest of mono or even PVDF—it stays put. For that reason you cannot expect to undo it very easily. This loop is known by several other names: Double Overhand Loop, the Two-Fold Water Knot, the Line Knot, and the Two-Fold Blood Knot. Nothing wrong with having a few extra names, just as long as you remember how to tie it, which is simplicity itself:

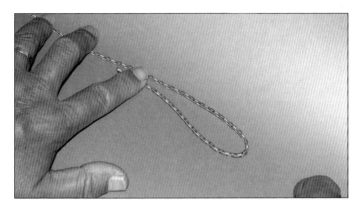

1 Make a loop.

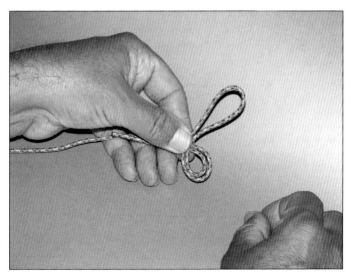

2 Start an overhand knot.

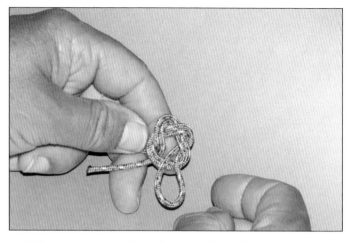

3 Make two passes through the overhand knot with the loop.

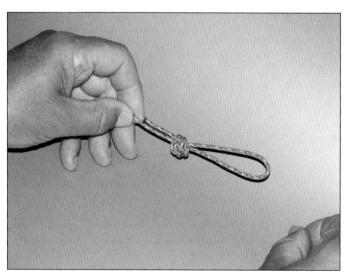

4 Pull tight—that's it.

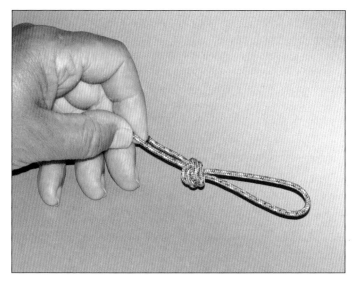

5 A view of the other side of the loop.

## Splicing a Loop in Dacron

Hollow-braided Dacron line is easy to splice provided that you have the right tools. Without them, you are very nearly sunk. The tools here came with a crimping set I have had for a while. I keep it pristinely clean, so that I do not have stray pieces of line, fluff, or other debris to get in the way of a nice, clean splice. You probably should make this at home, where you have plenty of light, a solid bench to work on, and maybe a beer handy for afterwards (NOT before). When you succeed with one splice, take a breather and get ready for however many more you need—make a production out of it. That way you won't have to fiddle around too much. Handy hint: Go to a craft store and get a lighted magnifying lens for this work—it makes it very much easier to do.

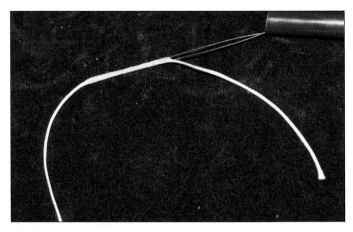

1 Insert the splicing needle into the end of your braid, about two inches from end A.

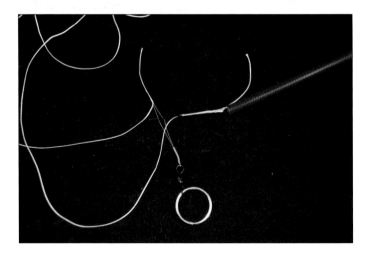

2 Run it through about two inches and exit through the side to pick up a threading tool, through which tool you insert the other end of your braid, end B.

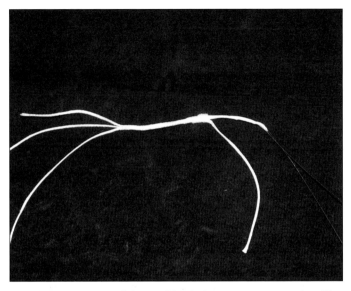

3 Now, run your splicing tool back the way you entered, pulling the end B of your braid with you to make a loop the size you need.

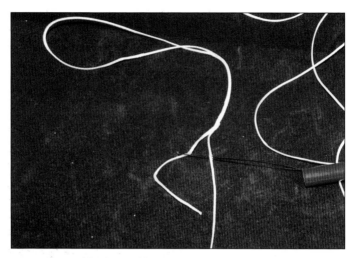

4 Smooth it all out and pass the splicing tool straight through the braid you just pulled through, about 1/4 inch below the exit point, and pick up the end A of the braid that you started with and pull it back through the braid.

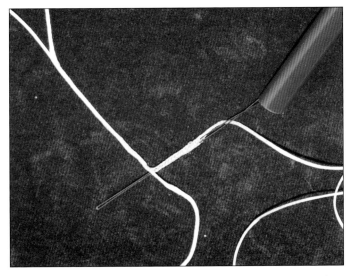

5 Insert the splicing tool into braid B, again about two inches away from the exit of end A, this time exiting the braid directly where end A comes out.

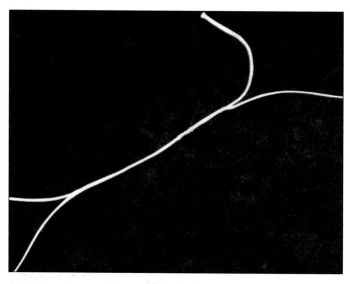

6 Now pull end A out of the end of the braided line and smooth out the line and loop.

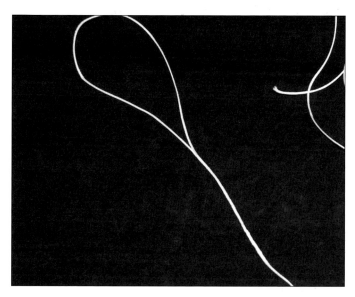

7 Nearly there. Cut away end A at the point where it exits, or even about 1/4 inch above where it comes out. Smooth out the loop and line again so that all is smooth and even.

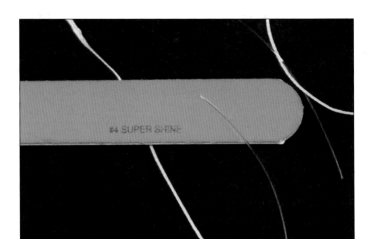

8 Now it is time to prepare the end of your monofilament leader. Using the finest smoother you have, remove all burrs from the end of the mono.

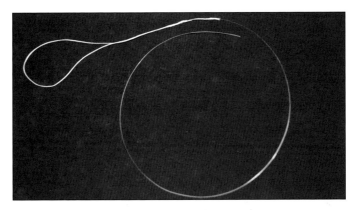

9 Insert the prepared leader end into the tail end of the spliced loop, until it reaches the A point of your braided loop. Add glue, smooth and straighten the connection and wait for it to dry. You are done.

# Chapter 6

# Knots for Fly-fishing

• *Albright Knot*   • *Bimini Twist*   • *Figure Eight Knot (with Orvis Loop Variation)*   • *Non-Slip Mono Loop*   • *Neater (Needle) Nail Knot*   • *Surgeon's Knot and Loop*   • *Trilene Knot* • *George Harvey Dry-Fly Knot*   • *Whipped Loop*

These nine knots represent a fair selection for fly-fishing. These are my favorites, and I think they represent the best. There is so much more to the subject that, if flies are your thing, do find other references on the subject (and there are a few recommendations among the bibliography) to gain a deeper understanding. These few will get you through most situations.

Many of these knots are described elsewhere in this book, in other chapters. That's where you'll find the illustrated tying instructions. Knots that are illustrated elsewhere will be limited in this chapter to a description of their application to fly-fishing. A couple of new ones, for fly-fishing in particular, will be illustrated here.

## Albright Knot

The Albright Knot (see Chapter 4) is used in fly-fishing for joining lines of dissimilar diameters or materials. This is the knot to use for fastening a single-strand stainless wire leader to a monofilament tippet. Likewise, it works for tying a heavy mono shock leader to the tippet.

## Bimini Twist

The Bimini Twist (Chapter 3) is used when you must maintain line strength at a connection. It can be tied in the end of the tippet to provide a doubled strand for fastening to the fly. It sees more use in construction of IGFA-legal leaders, where it is used to join the class tippet to a heavier shock tippet. Utilizing the double strands created by the Bimini Twist assures that the weakest part of the leader is the single strand of class tippet, which retains its full rated strength.

# Figure Eight Knot (with Orvis Loop Variation)

This knot is usually made in 10- to 60-pound-test braided wire and is seldom used any other place. The original Figure Eight is described in Chapter 2. The Orvis Loop variation is my own addition to the knot.

This photograph shows the finished Figure Eight with the cat's paw finish on the tag end, which brings the tag back parallel to the line, instead of leaving it pointing in the opposing direction.

# Non-Slip Mono Loop

You have already seen how to make this fine loop knot (Chapter 5), and I trust that you are making it correctly so as not to lose strength by slipping the tag through the wrong direction. This knot is useful for joining section of a mono leader, such as when attaching a leader to the line, or for building quick-change tippets. This knot works best when it is tailored to the material it is tied in. Here are some guidelines for getting the most out of this knot.

1. Make turns according to the weight of line:
    a. Up to 6-pound test—7 turns
    b. 8- to 12-pound test—5 turns
    c. 15- to about 40-pound test—3 turns
    d. Up to 60- (and over 40-)—2 turns
    e. Over 60-pound test monofilament—one turn only is needed


2. Lubricate the knot well with water before closing
3. Pull standing part and tag end well, alternating—it cannot be too tight.

# Neater (Needle) Nail Knot

We will cover variations of the Nail Knot in the next chapter, but this knot deserves discussion here for its importance as an essential fly-fishing knot. The Nail Knot, in one or more variations, is the time-honored method for joining a monofilament leader butt to the end of a modern, coated fly line.

This knot does not require a tube to make it—it can be built over anything—a toothpick, a straightened paper clip, or a needle to provide the stiffness around which to build the knot prior to tightening.

It is important in all variations to form up this knot carefully so the turns lie close together and do not overlap, then snug it slightly before withdrawing the stiffener.

Be careful to pull on both the tag end and the leader when tightening, to ensure that the whole knot is well formed and tight enough to bite into the fly-line coating. Withdraw the stiffener before tightening too much, or you will not be able to pull it out at all. Give the knot a good steady pull to seat it and test it, and then trim the tag end of the leader and the end of the fly-line closely so this knot will pass smoothly through the rod guides without catching. The knot and the two tag ends are commonly coated with Pliobond to make it even more streamlined

## Surgeon's Knot and Loop

This knot is useful for building loops to create quick-change leaders. The Surgeon's Loop (see Chapter 5) can be tied in the butt section of the leader, which can then be fastened with Interlocking Loops to the fly line or a short piece of monofilament permanently attached to the fly line with a Nail Knot. I have found that a simple hemostat end (nice and rounded) will help enormously in tightening when inserted into the Surgeon's Loop.

## Trilene Knot

One of the many knots (Chapter 3) that can be used for tying a fly to the tippet.

## George Harvey Dry-Fly Knot

This knot is designed to properly cock a dry fly on the surface, and as such should be used with turned-up-eye dry fly hooks. It is illustrated on a straight-eye hook for clarity, but if it is used with a straight-eye hook, the fly won't ride properly on the surface.

1 Take a counterclockwise turn through the eye of your fly and behind the standing part.

2 Make another turn, again from the front of the standing part to behind the first turn. Be sure to hold the turns against the standing part.

3 Make a wrap around the two turns.

4 Make a second wrap around the two turns.

5 Flip the two turns over the eye of the fly.

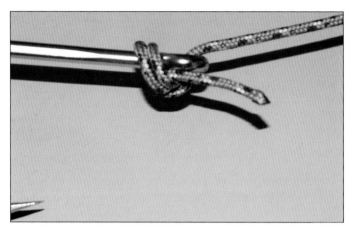

6 Pull tight. Don't forget to trim the tag end.

## Whipped Loop

This loop provides an alternative to the Nail Knot for fastening leaders to the end of the fly line, when the leader is to be joined to the line with a loop-to-loop connection. It is also the way to join multipart fly lines, such as shooting heads, or when using varying-density sink-tips that can be interchanged on the fly line. This loop in secured by serving the tag and standing parts of the line with lighter material, usually waxed nylon or dental tape. This loop takes time and patience, and should be made up ahead of time so it becomes part of the gear, rather than a knot you tie on the water.

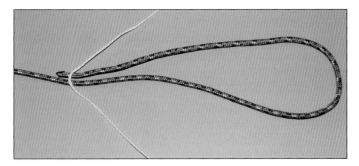

1 Bring the tag end parallel with the loop and prepare to wrap the whipping line.

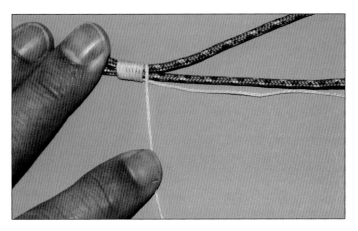

2 Leaving a long tag end (tag A), wrap around whipping line back over itself toward the loop, using about twelve turns.

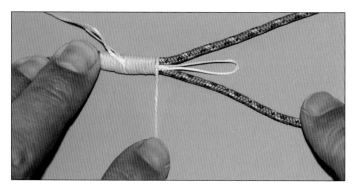

3 Lay a separate loop of whipping line or twine (Loop B) over the serving and continue wrapping the whipping line over the top of this loop.

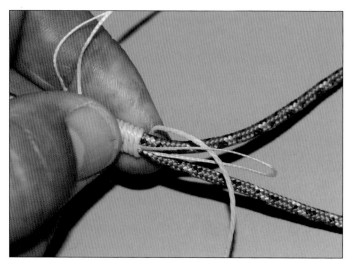

4 Bring the tag end of the whipping twine through Loop B from behind.

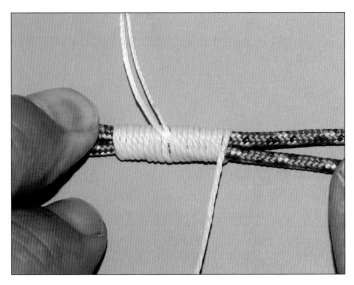

5 Pull on the other end of Loop B to capture the tag end of the whipping line tight against the wraps. Pull on the tag end of the whipping line to tighten the wraps. At this stage everything should be snug and stay in place.

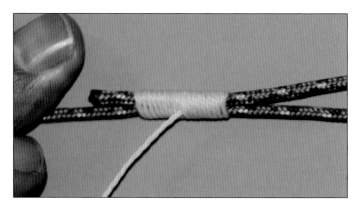

6 Pull on the ends of Loop B to pull the tag end under the wrapping loops, to exit between the wraps.

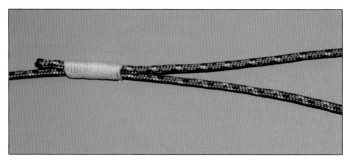

7 Trim the tag end of the whipping line closely. This serving can benefit from a coat of Pliobond to keep everything in place.

# Chapter 7

## Nail Knots—Now You'll Know

*· Tube Nail Knot · Emergency Nail Knot · Needle Nail Knot Alternative · Double Nail Knot · Nail Knot with a Loop*

Nail knots are generally used to secure a thin line to a thicker one with minimum bulk, so that the knot formed does not stick in the rod guides. The series is called nail knots because they used to be made with the aid of a fine carpentry nail—nowadays they are usually made with a small piece of brass or copper tubing. Tubing provides a stiffener for forming the wraps and allows the tag end to be easily inserted beneath the wraps easily, by running through the tube. In the illustrations, a plastic pen barrel has been used, for illustration and clarity. In practice, with smaller diameter lines, a smaller tube or stiffener is more appropriate.

# Tube Nail Knot

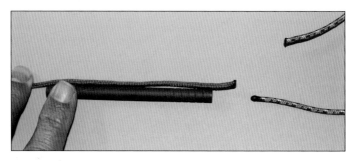

1 Bring the two lines toward each other, with opposing ends, laying your tube alongside the main line, and then bring your leader line alongside the tube.

2 Starting at the rod end, wrap the leader back down along itself, the tube, and the main line.

3 Having completed the wraps, take the tag end of the leader and pass it into the end of the tube.

4 Slide the tube out carefully, keeping firm hold (but not crushing) the wraps that were around the tube.

5 Roll the wraps with your fingers, bringing them snug to the main line, until you can hold the tag end and the standing part of the lighter line. Pull the tag end and the standing line to tighten the knot. Use flat-bladed pliers or hemostats if needed—the wraps MUST be tight or this will not work. Trim the leader tag and the butt end of your main line.

## Emergency Nail Knot

When you find yourself in need of a nail knot but without your handy tube or tool, use a loop of line in place of the tube. Simply replace the tube with a loop of Dacron or waxed whipping twine. Make the wraps toward the loop, and once the wraps are made, insert the tag end in the loop and withdraw the loop from beneath the wraps, pulling the tag end under them.

## Needle Nail Knot Alternative

This alternative is well suited for joining monofilament to braided Dacron or the end of a fly line. The mono is first inserted into the center of the heavier material, thus the needle, and exits through the side of the heavier line a 1/4 inch from the end. Then the knot is formed above the exit point. This configuration provides for extra strength, and a very smooth, snag-proof connection.

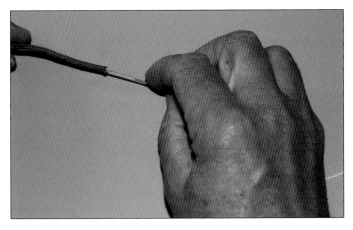

1 After trimming down or paring your monofilament with a razor blade and putting it on a needle, thread that needle into the end of your fly-line.

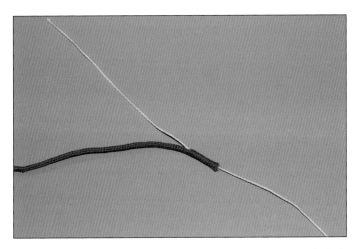

2 Push the needle in as far as you can, usually about 1/4 inch or so and remove the needle when the leader is in place.

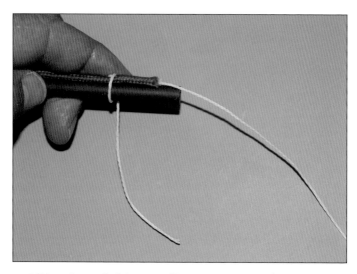

3 Wrap the end of the monofilament around the end of your fly-line, toward the butt end of your fly-line.

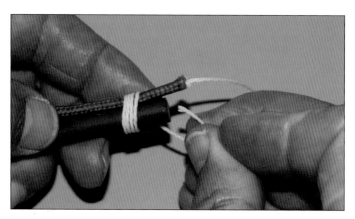

4 Insert the tag end of the leader into a fine tube or into the end of a separate but larger needle than you used in Stage 1 above.

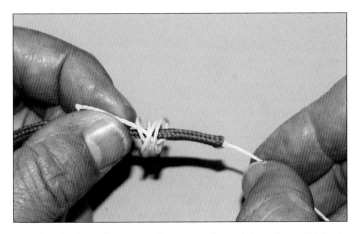

5 Gradually pull out the tube or needle and, keeping a tight grip on the wraps, start to fair them up by using your fingers to roll the wraps around the fly-line.

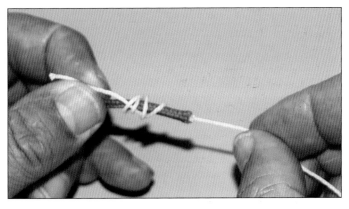

6 As you roll the wraps and pull the tag end, you will need to keep the wraps closer together.

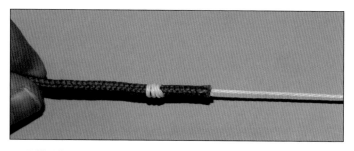

7 Finally, once the wraps are tight enough and you have tested the pull on the end of your leader to check it for security, you can cut away the leader tag and your needle nail knot is ready for use.

## Double Nail Knot

What is it about the Double Nail Knot that is so familiar? It looks outwardly like the Blood Knot, but it has a different structural action. This variation does not require a stiffener to form it. In some materials, this knot tends to work loose under pressure. If you tie it in monofilament, where the natural stretch of the line helps to bed the knot, it will hold two lines together securely.

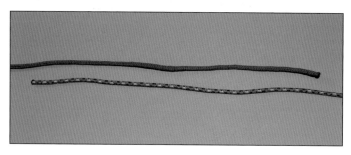

1 Lay your two lines toward each other, overlapping by about six inches.

2 Form an overhand, counterclockwise loop with one tag end.

3 Wrap the tag end around three to five times through the loop and pull the loop down snugly by pulling on the standing end.

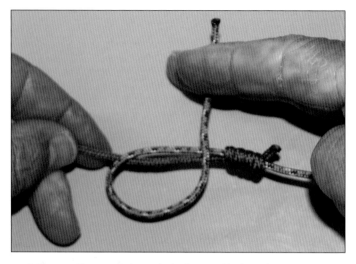

4 Repeat Stages 2 through 4 above with the other tag end.

5 Trim the tag ends and apply a coat of Pliobond.

## Nail Knot with a Loop

Sometimes it is better to have a loop that is adjustable, but that is not likely to slide unless you really strike it hard, and then it will slide just enough. This is just that knot. With careful adjustment of the tightness of the wraps, you can fine-tune this knot to a degree that other knots cannot achieve. Try it when you need your lure to swing freely, then have a snug connection during the ensuing fight.

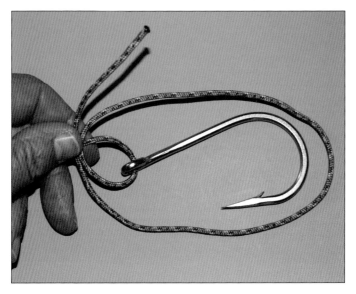

1 Form a clockwise loop, overhand, through the eye of your lure or hook, then a loop big enough to encompass the hook.

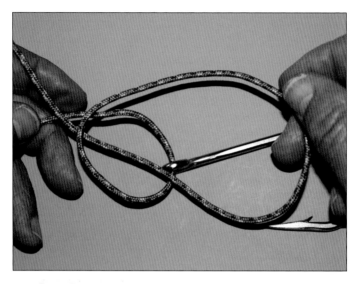

2 Pass the loop over your lure or hook (don't use triple hooks here or they are sure to catch the large loop) and start to wrap the tag and the main line.

3 Several turns later, depending on line choice, you have a smaller loop left to wrap, remembering to wrap over the lure or hook each time.

4 Now start to pull the tag end and firm up and fair the wraps, so that your nail knot starts to take shape.

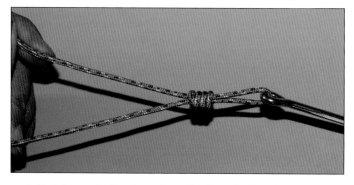

5 Pull the main line to reduce the loop to the size you want. Now, one last strong pull on the tag to make the wraps as tight as possible.

6 Trim the tag and you are good to go.

# Chapter 8

# Other Helpful Knots to Know

• *Paragum Knot*   • *Improved Turle Knot*   • *Whip Finish Snell*
• *World's Fair Knot*

We all need some knots to fall back on from time to time, when particular needs arise, and these knots are just that—a help when we just do not know what else to do. Try them for yourself and see if they can help you with taking care of small problems that arise.

## Paragum Knot

Really, this is just another name for the Double Grinner Knot, aka the Double Duncan, Shock Leader, Double Nail Knot, or the Barrel Knot. Use it whenever you need to secure two pieces of line together—it works equally well with mono and fluorocarbon line.

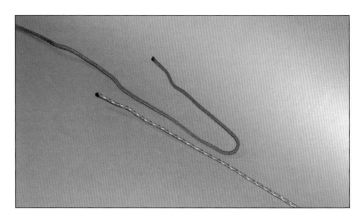

1 Lay the lines alongside each other, overlapping and with one end in a bight.

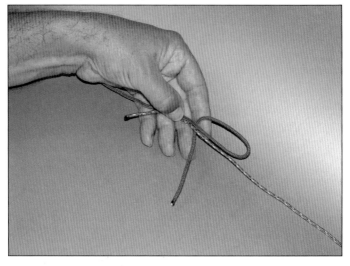

2 Wrap the left line behind the bight, keeping the bight a little open.

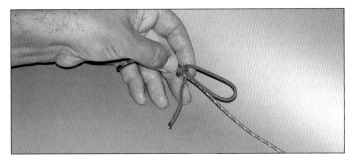

3 Continue wrapping the tag end around one leg of the bight.

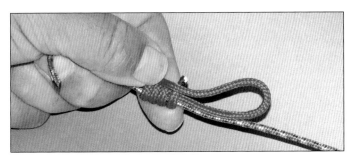

4 Wrap for four wraps, tucking the tag end under the other leg of the bight.

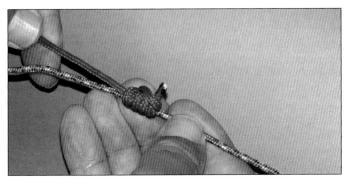

5 Pull on the standing part to close the bight against the tag end.

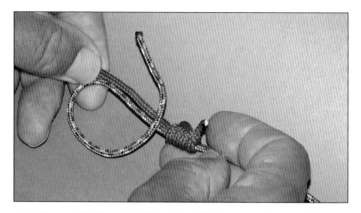

6 Form a bight against the line with the second tag end.

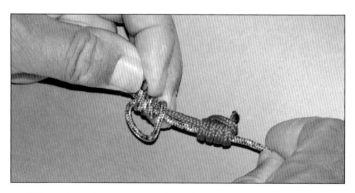

7 Complete the same number of turns around the near leg of the bight.

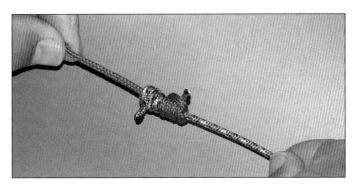

8 Roll the two wrapped parts toward each other carefully, so as not to lose the turns you put in, and pull each standing part to bring the two wrappings together tightly.

## Improved Turle Knot

The Improved Turle Knot (sometimes mistakenly referred to as the Turtle Knot) is probably one of the least appreciated knots. The original Turle was developed for organic lines, and it didn't work as well in monofilament. The improved version works just fine with mono, and the knot helps to keep the fly in line with the tippet, which is its best feature.

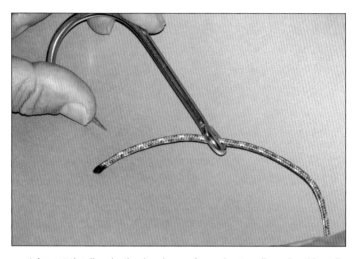

1 Insert the line in the hook eye from the top (imagine it's a fly hook, instead of the shark hook I have used).

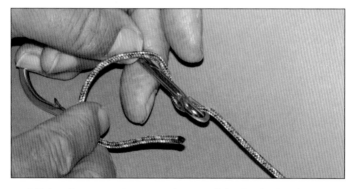

2 Bring the tag end up over the top of the hook shank.

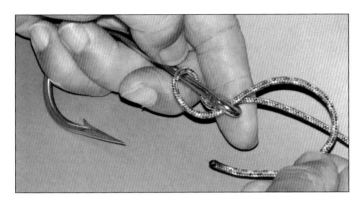

3 Bring the tag end back up through the eye.

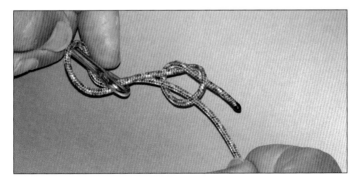

4 Form a left-hand overhand knot around the standing part, so that tag end and standing part both exit the knot on the same side.

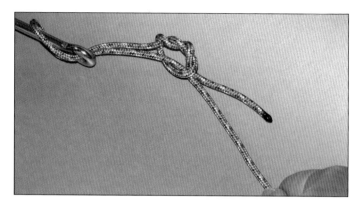

5 Make a second pass of the tag end to form a double overhand knot.

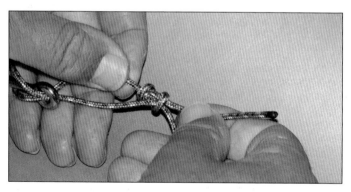

6 Snug the double overhand together and pass half into the hook eye.

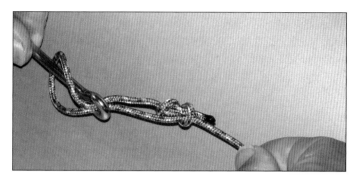

7 Now start to ease and fair the loop around the fly head to bring the tippet into firm contact.

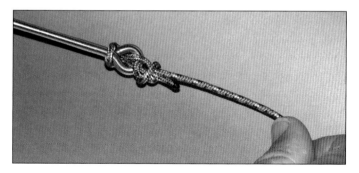

8 Pull firmly on the standing part of the tippet, to snug the double overhand well into the eye for a firm hold, in-line with your tippet material.

## Whip Finish Snell

Snelling, which is a variation of Whip Finishing, looks very similar to something I learned to do when working on tall ships, except that there we used marline or seine twine, which is quite a bit stronger than fishing line, and we made all the turns with a marlinespike and called it serving a line. Basically this knot wraps the line around the shank of the hook to hold it in place. You do not need a marlinespike to do this—for fishing line all you need are your hands. Be sure to follow the advice of sailors from times past—keep the wraps tight, and tight against each other.

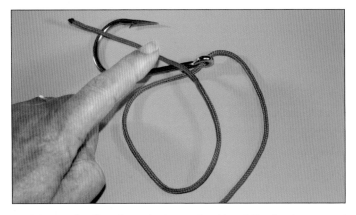

1 Insert the line through the underside of the hook eye and form a counterclockwise loop along the shank of the hook.

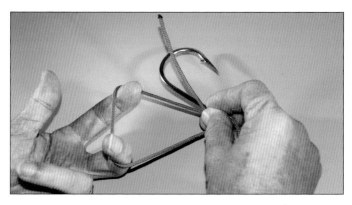

2 Hold hook eye and the line where it crosses itself in one hand. Insert the fingers of the other hand facing up, into the loop, as shown.

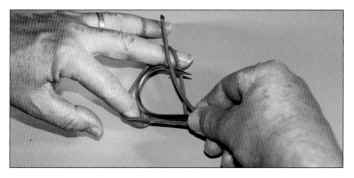

3 Roll your hand toward you and pass the loop under the bend of the hook.

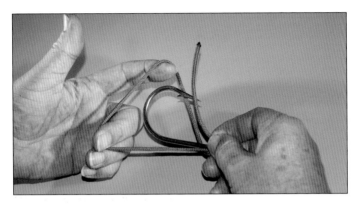

4 Roll your hand again so the index finger wraps the standing line part of the loop around the hook shank and the tag end. The wraps will pass under the shank and away from you, then back over the top toward you. This is a difficult choreography at first— just remember, you are wrapping the standing side of the loop around the tag-end side of the loop and the hook shank.

5 Repeat the wraps until you have five or six turns around the hook shank.

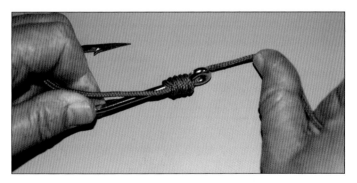

6 Hold the wraps and the tag so the knot does not unwind and pull on the standing end to snug the wraps and pull them tightly around the hook shank.

The tightened knot will hold the shank securely, behind the eye of the hook. Trim the tag end and you are done.

## World's Fair Knot

This knot, by Mr. Gary Martin of Indiana, won first prize in the DuPont World's Fair Knot search of nearly 500 entries. The writers judging the contest were looking for the easiest-to-tie new knot for all-purpose fishing. Gary came up with the name because he was demonstrating it at the 1982 World's Fair in Knoxville, Tennessee. Easy to tie, secure and useful to attach to a hook, bobber, sinker, or lure, with any line except wire.

1 Insert a loop through the eye, keeping the point of the hook as shown.

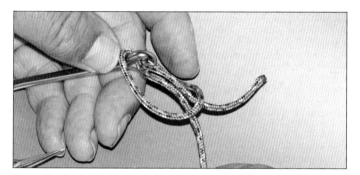

2 Fold the loop back over the eye, tag end, and the standing part.

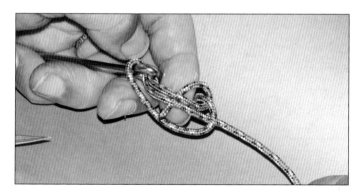

3 Bring the tag end around in a loop toward the eye, pushing the tag end through the folded loop and under the standing parts.

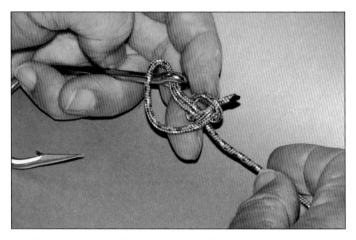

4 Tuck the tag end back up through its own loop.

5 Finally fair up the knot to the eye by pulling the standing part firmly, adjusting the loops as you fair the knot gradually.

# Chapter 9

# Building Terminal Rigs

*• Leaders for Fly Fishing    • Dropper Loop    • Fish-Finder Rig*
*• Adding a Leader Anywhere with the Longliner's Knot*
*• Shock Leader*

## Leaders for Fly Fishing

### A Basic Formula

There are many different formulas for building fly leaders, and many specialized variations. The wise approach is to start with a sound formula that works for you, then customize it as needed for special situations. The different lengths of mono in a tapered leader are traditionally joined with a Blood Knot or Surgeon's Knot. For specialized leaders, other knots may come into play, but start with the basics.

There are a couple of fundamental leader constructions that have proven their worth. The first is a general-purpose formula that is adaptable for both fresh and salt water, as developed by Lefty Kreh.

Kreh's advice is to taper a leader by reducing the length of each section by half of the length of the previous section. Using this structure, you'd begin with a 4-foot section of 25-pound line followed by a 2-foot section 20-pound line of the next diameter, then a 12-inch section of 15-pound line and, finally a 6-inch section of 12-pound for the final taper, finishing with a 2-foot tippet matched to the fly. Sounds good to me—if it ain't broke, let's not try to fix it.

## A Specialized Dry Fly Leader

The George Harvey dry fly leader uses more specific instructions, and is based on monofilament diameters, in various stiffnesses, to create a leader tuned to its task.

The formula is:

.017-inch diameter mono for the first 10 inches
Hard nylon for the next three sections:
.015-inch for 20 inches
.013-inch for 20 inches and
.011-inch for 20 inches
Soft nylon for the last section of
.009-inch for 12 inches
.008-inch for 18 inches
.007-inch for 22 to 28 inches

You can make a longer leader by cutting back the final section of .007 to about 18 inches and adding a section of .006-inch material for 22 to 28 inches for the tippet.

## Using Wire

Wire bite tippets prevent the fish with teeth from biting through the nylon tippet after they have taken the fly. You may elect to use a Monel or stainless wire. Pike require a long length of wire—probably about two feet—whereas others, mackerel for example, will get spooked by such a long wire, and you should limit the length to about six inches or so. When you are fishing under IGFA rules, of course, you are going to be constrained by those requirements for terminal tackle, so read the rules before building your leaders. When attaching wire, use the Albright Knot in combination with a Haywire Twist for solid wire and an Albright with a Huffnagle for braided wire.

# Dropper Loop

The dropper loop enables you to add an additional hook anywhere along your line, without having to resort to specialized equipment that you may not have on hand. It also enables you to select and remove the loop without too much work. It is a relatively straightforward knot to make—just remember to grip the two legs firmly in your fingers as you make it and all will be well.

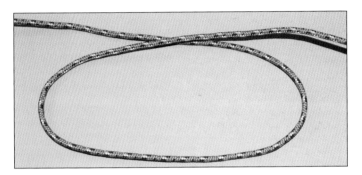

1 Form an overhand clockwise loop.

2 Flip the loop upwards by gripping the line on each side with your thumb and middle fingers and pushing up with your pointing fingers.

3 Keep rotating the loop around towards you until . . .

4 You form a "mouth" in the middle and can insert the remainder of the loop into the "mouth."

5 Tighten all the turns on each side of the "mouth" and pull the loop down to tighten.

6 Ready for action.

## Fish-Finder Rig

The name "Fish-Finder Rig" is not mine, nor does it belong to any individual I know, although it does have an entry in McClane's *The Wise Fisherman's Encyclopedia* from 1951, so I guess it must be at least in part attributable to Vlad Evanoff, who was the editor of that article. Yet it is used all the time to describe the bottom-bait construction that is described here. Principally used when surf-fishing, such as in the Outer Banks of North Carolina, it is used to hold the bait near the bottom while still allowing the line to play out through the sinker. As the line pays out on the strike you can feel it, but the fish feels no resistance from the sinker. Various types of sinkers are used in different locations, for different types of bottom, so seek local advice on this. Here is how to put one together:

Run your fishing line through a sinker so it slides freely, and attach a swivel to the end of the line. The swivel should be large enough to act as a stopper for the sinker. To the other loop of the swivel, tie the leader, and tie the other end of the leader to the hook.

With this setup, the sinker and bait stays on the bottom, but the fish can pick up the bait and move off without being spooked by the feeling the resistance of the sinker. This is the most basic of Fish-Finder Rigs. Local conditions determine the size and shape of the sinker. As well, there are any number of specialized components developed for specific species and locations. They may or may not be useful, but check with local shops where you plan to fish for information on favored local practices and gear. Armed with an understanding of how a basic Fish-Finder Rig works, you can easily adapt it as required.

## Adding a Leader Anywhere with the Longliner's Knot

This knot is known as the Longliner's Knot, and is used to add a leader or dropper (also known as a snood) to monofilament line. It has the added benefit of being fully able to attach anywhere along your line without your having to have a swivel ready to use. You may also add more than one at a time. Be sure that you only use a lighter line than the main line to make this knot.

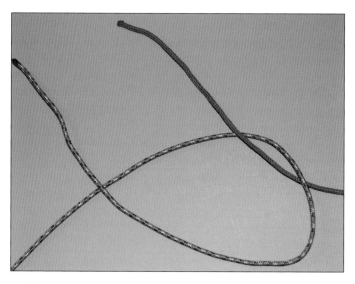

1 Form an overhand clockwise loop in your main line and insert the leader line up into it.

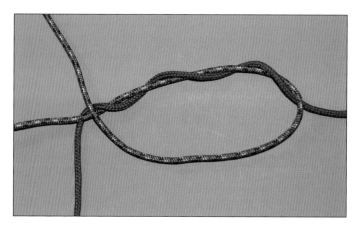

2 Wind the leader around one leg of the main line loop.

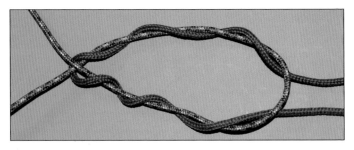

3 Continue around the other leg of the main line loop until you return to the start of your leader entry point.

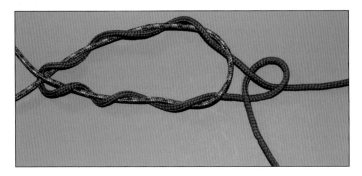

4 Make a half hitch around the leader.

5 Make a second turn around the leader and finish with an overhand knot through both half hitches.

6 Pull the leader down tight, making the turns around the main line come closer together.

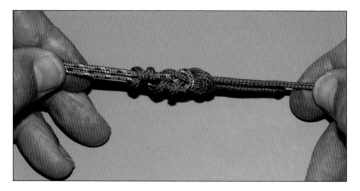

7 Adjust the leader turns around the main line from the leader knot backwards, so that the final leader knot is next to the main line loop end.

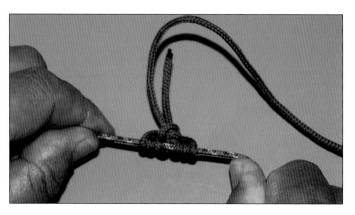

8 Grasp the main line firmly (use gloved hands for any line over 15-pound test) and pull it straight.

9 Slide the knot by gripping it firmly and pushing it to the place you need the dropper.

# Shock Leader

A shock leader is simply a way of adding stronger material above the hook to prevent the fish from biting or abrading the line. You could use wire, but it tends to be a bit heavy and stiff, and will spook some fish, depending on what you are after and whether you are trolling or fly-fishing. Of the many ways of making the shock leader, these two are my favorites.

**Method 1**
Use the Double Nail Knot (aka Double Grinner) shown in a previous chapter. It is quick and easy to tie and seldom lets go. It is the preferred method for a really secure attachment when you are fishing for larger, more active fish, like tarpon.

**Method 2**
The second method relies on successfully bringing two knots together, so that they engage together and form a strong bond, helped along with a dab of Pliobond or an epoxy adhesive. Be aware, however, that this knot is probably more suited to fly-fishing than to trolling for larger fish.

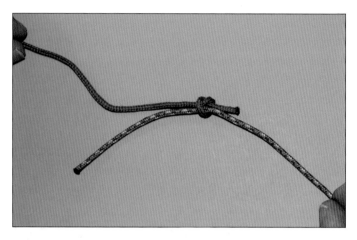

1 Tie an overhand knot around the leader line with the main line.

2 Form an overhand counterclockwise loop with the leader, over the top of the main line.

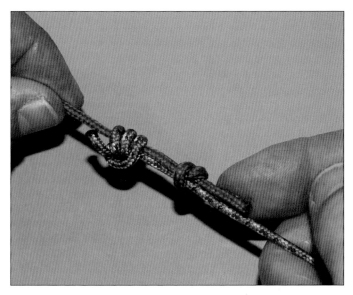

3 Wrap the leader three times around the main line and tuck back through.

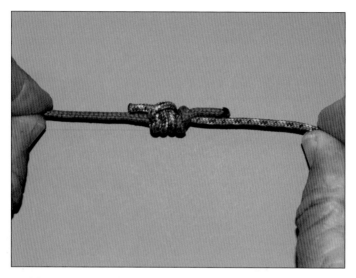

4 Fair up both knots and pull both standing parts together.

# Chapter 10

# Last Thoughts

- *Shock Cords*  - *Shoelaces*  - *Lanyard for License*
- *The Best Spectra Knot*

All those useful knots for tying line to bait, arbor, leader, sinker, and bobber—you probably know enough to deal with anything now, don't you? I always think about more knots when I come across new, challenging situations, and I want to pass along a few helpful knots that I have used very handily in the past. These are not necessary to catch fish, but they certainly add to the experience.

## Shock cords

Shock cords seem to have a mind of their own—just when you could swear you have tied a knot in one, it works its way loose and you are left with a flapping tarp or you have lost a vital part of your load. This is where the Perfection Loop (see Chapter 5) comes into play. Use this knot when you need to secure a shock cord, and the loop will stay put.

## Shoelaces

Shoelaces are an important element of fishing, whether it is to keep your laces from tripping you up on a slippery boat deck, or lacing up your wading shoes securely for a day in the river.

This is my favorite shoelace knot—nothing else I have seen or used does the job nearly as well as this one.

Be aware that you may have to tug a little more to get the knot undone, but the extra security is worth the effort.

1 Tie a regular overhand knot, just like always.

2 Take the left side lace, make it into a loop, and then take the right side lace and pass it once over your thumb and forefinger holding the loop.

3 Tricky part here—pass the right side lace around your thumb and forefinger a second time.

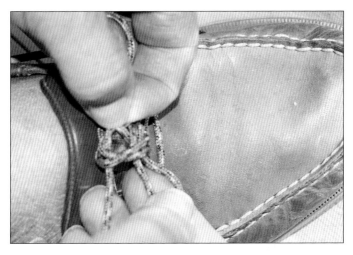

4 Push a bight of the right side lace through the two passes that are around your thumb to make the new left side loop.

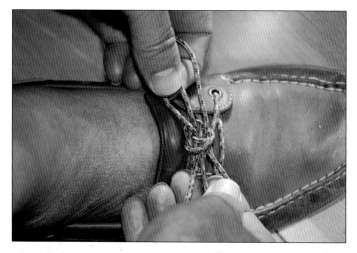

5 Pull both loops out to the sides. Notice that the wraps in the center cross over each other quite naturally—they are supposed to—it's what makes the knot so tight the laces will not easily come undone, even if you snag the loops on something.

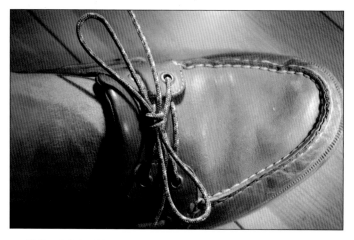

6 The finished knot.

# Lanyard for License

As a final, slightly more fancy touch, some winter evening put together this handy license holder lanyard. Finished with a hook and a plastic envelope, the lanyard, which takes less than an evening to make, will last for years, look elegant, and you'll always know right where your license is.

1 Tie four pieces of cord, each about five feet long, together in the center. I have used a Constrictor Knot, but feel free to use your own favorite. Make two pairs of lines like here . . .

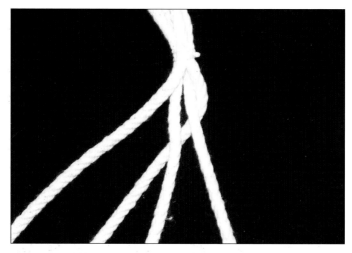

2 Take the outer RH string and pass it behind the two middle ones.

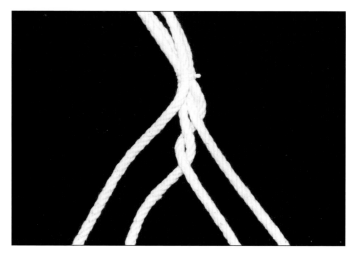

3 Return that string to its own pair, but now it forms the inner one of the two.

4 Take the outer LH string and bring it behind the middle two . . .

5 Return it to its own pair, again forming the inner one of the two . . .

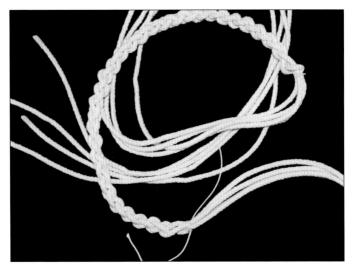

6 Repeat 2 through 5 as many times as you care, making sure to keep the pattern even. When you get to about the last six inches or so, put on another stop-knot of your choosing (you could even use a rubber band if you like) . . .

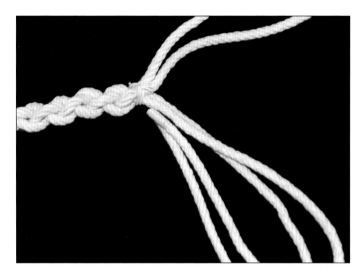

7 You guessed it—go back to the middle of all your cords and start again, but in the opposite direction. Do be sure to take off your temporary knot around the middle of the cords before proceeding.

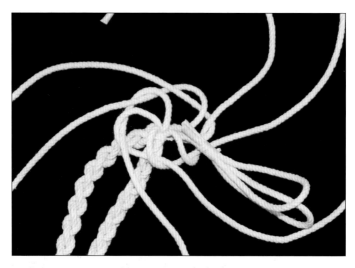

8 If you are comfortable with this length of cord around your neck and want to stop, simply make a double or single loop, tie the rest of the cords together, and hang your plastic license holder there. For those who want something more, we are now going to make a wall and crown knot. Take two cords and whip them together to form a loop. These two cord loops stay in the center of the knot. Take the remaining six cords and arrange them like the spokes of a wheel (hold the pair of braided cords in your hand). Tuck each of the cords under its neighbor to the left, then take that neighbor cord and tuck it in turn under its neighbor to the left, until you get to the first tuck you made, then pass the sixth cord end up through the loop you formed when you made that first tuck. Your cords should look like the diagram.

8A Here it is in close-up.

9 We just made wall knots, so now we are going to make the crown knots. Walls go up and crown rhymes with down, so we make the cord ends go down instead of up. Here is how it starts . . .

9A . . . and here is how it looks when it is done.

10 Follow the cord around the knot from the cord it lies next to, as shown here, using a hollow fid to help you lead the cord through. Because we are doubling the cords, we are now making a second wall alongside the first wall.

11 Now we follow each crown down. Look at the cord loop in the middle of the photo. Its end is coming out of the bottom of the knot just to the right of where it enters the top.

11A Now we have all six cords entering the top of the knot, ready to be pulled down into place. Notice the four cords of the double loop at the right of the photograph. Once you have pulled down all the crown ends, cut them off next to the underside of the knot.

12 Now your lanyard is complete. Finish it to your own liking—this one I have left unfinished, but you could coat it with wax or varnish. If you varnish cotton, it gets fuzzy if you don't seal it with lacquer first. Or you could just leave the cords natural.

## The Best Spectra Knot

I picked this knot up from a fisherman on the pier one day. I have tried it in slipperier line than the notorious Spectra and it holds just fine.

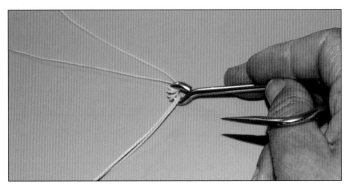

1 Wrap a bight through the eye of your hook three times.

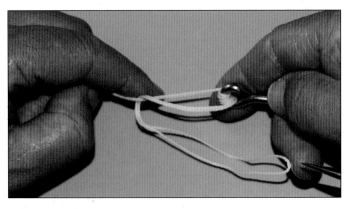

2 Wrap the bight four times back over itself toward the hook eye.

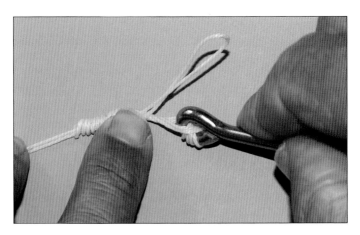

3 Open the wraps around the eye by opening them up with a splicing tool or needle.

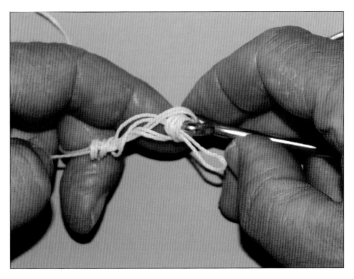

4 Pass the bight back through the wraps.

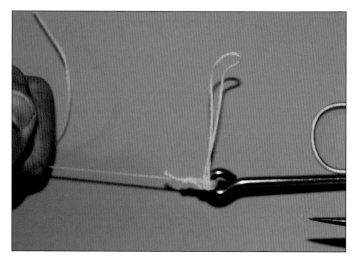

5 Pull the standing part of the line, to close the wraps around the eye and the wraps around the standing part. You will now have to give a tug to the bight as it exits the eye wraps.

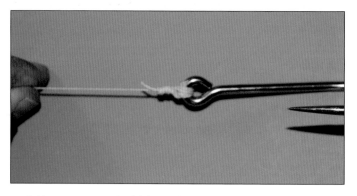

6 Now cut away the bight and the tag end of the original loop for your finished hitch. Coat if needed with Pliobond or epoxy adhesive.

# Glossary

A few terms you may come across in this book, on your next fishing trip, or in your favorite fishing magazine:

**Arbor** The center or axle of the reel spool.

**Backing Line** The line fixed to the arbor (see above) to work as your backing in case you run out of leader and line, or to use as filer when using expensive specialty line, such as Monel or Spectra, where filling the spool with it does not serve any purpose.

**Breaking Strain or Breaking Strength (BS)** The nominal strength, usually expressed in pounds, of a piece of line. Nominal strength is usually the average strength of a series of tests on the line.

**Butt** The end of the rod or line.

**Copolymer** A plastic made from a mixture of polymers (other plastics) to form a mix that performs better (is stronger or more elastic or has better abrasion resistance) than any of the polymers by themselves.

**Eye** The ring at the end of a hook or lure for attaching the leader or line.

**Fiber** Something flexible that is used to make a fishing line.

**Fluorocarbon** A compound used to make incredibly strong, thin leaders and lines.

**Fly**   Depending on your point of view, a pest or a useful end to your line that hides a hook with which you hope to catch a fish when fly fishing. The actual bait is artificial, designed to look like an insect or a baitfish.

**Fly Fishing**   Angling or fishing for fish, using a fly (lure) that is designed to look like an insect or other natural bait that fish feed on.

**Fly Line**   A line that is used for fly-fishing, usually tapered.

**Handline**   A line typically used when shore fishing, or when crabbing off the rocks as a kid, the spool of which is a rectangular handle, around which the line is wound. The spool is held in one hand, and the other end with the hook and float and/or sinker is whirled around the head and cast out to where you want the bait to be. The line comes off the spool as it trails out over the water, and you bring it in by winding line back onto the spool turn by turn.

**IGFA**   The International Game Fishing Association.

**IGKT**   The International Guild of Knot Tyers, founded in 1982.

**Lanyard**   A loop of line used to attach to something you don't want to lose overboard, like your camera, license, or net.

**Leader** A supplementary piece of line between the fishing line and the hook. The tapered length of monofilament line fastened to the fly-line, to which the fly is attached. May be tapered by knotting progressively thinner pieces, or tapered by manufacturer.

**Line**   The flexible stuff that connects your arbor to your hook or leader. Keep it dry and replace it every year or so.

**Loop**   A bend in a piece of line where the parts of the line cross each other to close a circle.

**Lure**   Something artificial that looks tasty or interesting to a fish.

**Monofilament**   A line that is made of a single strand, extruded or pultruded.

**Monomer**   A molecule with relatively low molecular weight (light) that can combine with other similar molecules to form polymers. Styrene and ethylene are monomers.

**Multifilament** Having more than two monofilaments. Usually a braided or bonded line made of polyethylene, sometimes known as Super Line. Can be five or ten times stronger that an equivalent steel line thickness. Cost is four or five times greater than monofilament and it will require much more line to fill a spool or reel.

**Nettle** A bundle of line made in such a way that you can just pull one end and have it all feed out of the bundle, while the rest of the bundle stays together. Handier than a spool sometimes and less likely to fall apart.

**Polymer** Usually high molecular weight (heavier) materials such as plastics that have repeating base sub-units. Polystyrene and polyethylene are polymers (see Monomer above).

**Polyvinylidenefluoride (PVDF)** A fluoropolymer, sometimes known as Kynar or Hylar. A strong, usually clear, plastic line.

**Reel** Mechanical device that holds fishing line, often employing a ratchet feed or braking system, but sometimes much simpler.

**Seat/Seated** When your knot has fully engaged all its turns, it is said to be seated or faired.

**Shank** The part of your hook that connects the business end or point (bill or barb) of the hook to the eye or spade end where the line is attached.

**Sinker** The heavy weight you attach to your line to make it sink.

**Snell** Literally, to wrap neatly. Usually used in connection of line to the shank of your hook, to prevent the fish from biting through the line.

**Spade End** The flattened end of your hook, used instead of an eye (see above).

**Standing Part** The part of your line that mostly stands still, attached to the arbor. The opposite end from the tag or working end (see below).

**Stopper Knot** A knot designed to stop the line from moving beyond the point where it is tied. See Overhand Knot and Figure Eight Knot.

**Swivel**  A mechanical device that allows your line, lure, hook, or other gear to rotate about its own center, sometimes having low-friction mating surfaces, sometimes fitted with ball-bearings, thereby preventing twist in your lines.

**Tag End**  The end of your line or leader that is usually snipped away after tying a knot. Curiously, there may be a tag end on your arbor, where it attaches on the standing part of your line.

**Tippet**  The finest end part of your fly leader to which the fly or shock tippet is attached.

**Turn**  Term used to describe a single rotation of line around the standing part. Also used to describe a complete circle made with the tag end of the line when tying on a hook.

**Weir**  A barrier in a body of water used to control the flow of water. Sometimes used to describe a wattle or wicker fence placed in the stream flow to help catch fish by diverting the fish into a trap.

**Working End**  Term used sometimes to describe the part of a line that is used to make a knot—it is the part that is moving or doing the work when tying the knot. See also Tag End above.

**Wrap**  Term used to describe a turn (see above) or used by moviemakers to describe the successful end of a piece of work—like this glossary.

# Bibliography

Ashley, Clifford Warren, *The Ashley Book of Knots* (Doubleday, Doran & Company, Inc., New York, 1944)

Kreh, Bernard "Lefty," Mark Sosin, *Practical Fishing Knots* (The Lyons Press, 1991)

Kreh, Bernard "Lefty," *Fly Fishing Knots and Connections* (The Lyons Press, an imprint of the Globe Pequot Press, Guilford, Connecticut, 2004)

McClane, A.J., Editor, *McClane's Standard Fishing Encyclopedia and International Angling Guide* (Holt, Rinehart and Winston, New York, 3rd printing, 1972)

McNally, Tom, compiled by Bob McNally, *Tom McNally's Complete Book of Fishermen's Knots* (Van Nostrand Reinhold Ltd, Scarborough, Ontario, 1975)

Miles, Tony, Ford, Martin and Gathercole, Peter, *The Complete Encyclopedia of Fishing* (Lorenz Books, an imprint of Anness Publishing Ltd., London, 2005)

Owen, Peter, *The Field Stream Fishing Knots Handbook* (The Lyons Press, Guilford, Connecticut, an imprint of the Globe Pequot Press, 2nd ed., 2006)

Sigler, Cam, *Guide to Fly Fishing* (Stackpole Books, Harrisburg, Pa., 1991)

Wilson, Geoff, *Encyclopedia of Fishing Knots and Rigs* (Australian Fishing Network, Victoria, Australia, 2003)

# Index